Why Flip a Coin?

Why Flip a Coin?

The Art and Science of Good Decisions

H. W. Lewis

John Wiley & Sons, Inc.

New York ■ Chichester ■ Weinheim ■ Brisbane
Singapore ■ Toronto

Copyright © 1997 by H. W. Lewis. All rights reserved
Published by John Wiley & Sons, Inc.
Published simultaneously in Canada

This publication is designed to provide accurate and authoritative
information in regard to the subject matter covered. It is sold with the
understanding that the publisher is not engaged in rendering professional
services. If professional advice or other expert assistance is required, the
services of a competent professional person should be sought.

Library of Congress Cataloging-in-Publication Data:

Lewis, H. W. (Harold Warren)
    Why flip a coin? : the art and science of good decisions
 / H.W. Lewis
    p.   cm.
    Includes index.
    ISBN 0-471-29645-7 (paper)
    1. Decision-making. I. Title.
BF448.L48 1997
153.8'3—dc20   98-29444
                                             CIP

Printed in the United States of America

10 9 8 7 6 5 4 3

Contents

Introduction

There is no known way to escape decision making. Sometimes among pleasures and sometimes not. Sometimes in our professional or business lives, sometimes not. Sometimes for profit or advancement, sometimes not. Sometimes because we decide it's time to make a decision, sometimes because it is forced upon us. Whatever the reason, it makes sense to do the job well instead of depending on luck, which means it pays to understand how decisions are made. This is a book about how to make decisions with skill, and toward the end it is a book about how governments can (and increasingly cannot) make decisions. It will not teach you how to avoid mistakes for the rest of your life—that's asking too much. Besides, there is no foolproof way to tell, *at the time of the decision,* whether the one you've just made will turn out to have been wonderfully right or horribly wrong, or (as often as not) soon forgotten. For the final scorecard we have to wait until the consequences are played out, however long it takes. Sometimes we never find out, or even care, because a decision that once seemed critical may become a vague memory before the clock strikes three. Things change.

On top of that, the final outcome is a bad way to judge how well we did at the time of the decision. If something we couldn't possibly have foreseen happens, it isn't fair to have to take the blame if the surprise is bad, and it isn't honest to take the credit if it is good. Luck, good and bad, comes to all of us. If we decide to go for a hike on a beautiful day in the springtime, and end up getting bombed by a passing bird, that doesn't mean the decision to hike was a bad one. Things happen.

So what we mean by a good decision is a decision that is the best we can do with what we know at the time. If we have done our best, *and* have been rational in our thinking, we will have done all that can be expected. What is out of our control is out of our control.

The need for decisions greets us every morning, and never rests. We decide what to have for breakfast, until we develop habits. We decide whether to make an impulse purchase at a checkout stand at a supermarket. We decide whether and when to get married (or our potential spouse lets us believe we are making a decision). We decide whether to go to the movies, go for a walk, buy a car, diaper the baby, finish the spinach, put a chip on red or black in a game of roulette, take or quit a job, write a book, or even read a book. Whatever your reasons, conscious or not, well considered or not, you have decided to start reading this book. That was a decision.

For a personal decision, with the power of choice and the bearer of the consequences all wrapped up in one individual, there is a "best way" to do the job, though we can't be expected to do our best all the time. More often we muddle through life making impulsive decisions, some good and some not so good, and only occasionally do we even remember later whether we were right or wrong. (Unless it was a memorable occasion, either way, who remembers the decisions that went into last Thursday's lunch?) Sometimes it does matter, and then we may end up either patting ourselves on the back or fantasizing about what might have been. Robert Browning and John Greenleaf Whittier each wrote famous poetry about that. "It once might have been, once only . . ."

And people differ. There are those who will try anything—they are rash, daring, adorable, and the heroes of popular fiction and television. The word *reckless* means without reckoning—without thinking. (The reckless heroes of fiction are usually protected by the author from the consequences of their daring. They jump from high places without a scratch to show for it. Real life is less forgiving.) Other folks live in an agony of endless indecision, hunkering down and fearful of error, but never really accomplishing anything worth remembering. "Gather ye rosebuds while ye may," said Robert Herrick; take a chance. Still others make only extremely conservative decisions, avoiding error at all costs, and also never really accomplishing anything memorable. Government bureaucrats are infamous for this character defect. There's plenty of room between the extremes.

The going gets tougher when there are more participants sharing the costs of bad decisions, more reaping the benefits of good ones, and more participating in the decision. You can have any combination of deciders and targets, many or few for either role. The first serious effort to understand multiplayer decision making was in the context of competitive team games, where better decisions can translate directly into winning. Despite all the empty lectures our children get about playing just for the fun of it, people who play games do like to win. Games have been played throughout human history—children prepare for adult life by playing imitative games—and some people are simply better at thinking games than others. (Different sports offer different roles for intelligent decision making, and not always very important roles. In basketball and sumo wrestling, a small genius always loses.)

The strategy of war involves game theory, and the prize for making better decisions than your opponent may be your own survival or the survival of your family, tribe, or country. It pays to practice before the stakes get that high, and that's what most games are all about. Fencing, boxing, polo, chess, javelin throwing, go, wrestling—these all develop combative skills. Wellington is supposed to have said (rightly or wrongly is not for us to judge) that the battle of Waterloo was won on the playing fields of Eton. The great military strategists are good at thinking ahead through several possible moves and countermoves, like good chess players, and the best of them (in practice the survivors) often end up writing about how they did it. (The winners write about their own genius, but the losers rarely write about what they did wrong. Generals usually have better reputations than they deserve—for every winner, there is a loser.) Modern soldiers-in-training read these books and study these old battles, but there are only a few general principles to guide a beginner. There are, of course, slogans born of ancestral experience: "Take the High Ground," "Divide and Conquer." But there is little theory. (One of the few general principles of warfare, Lanchester's law, is familiar to pitifully few professional military people. We'll give it a short chapter later.) That's why, with only one genuine exception known to this author, armies facing a real war start out with the same strategy and tactics used in the previous war, whether they won or lost the last time around. During the Hundred Years' War, the French army was decisively defeated by English longbowmen at Crécy in 1346, again at Poitiers in 1356, and once again at Agincourt in 1415. They were slow learners, and it cost them dearly. The French language even has a term, *arme blanche*—literally, "a clean weapon"—to describe a cutting weapon like a sword, presumably because the nobility once thought that killing at long range with archery or guns was ungentlemanly. Perhaps so, but weapons with a long reach are mighty effective against swords and lances—Leo Durocher is supposed to have said that nice guys finish last. The United States has not done all that well at innovation or at winning battles since World War II, except when we could overwhelm the opposition with men and materiel. That is usually a winning strategy, regardless of skill. If a genius stands up to a tank driven by a dunderhead, bet on the tank.

Real multiparty decision making comes in many forms, some with multiple players but only one side (ideal committees), others with two players and two sides (wrestling, chess, fencing, or singles tennis), and still others with multiple players and multiple sides (Congress, the United Nations, poker, or any of our political parties). At the highest level there is the struggle of the human race for long-term survival on Earth, let alone a decent quality of life. Monumentally important decisions need to be made and implemented, but a rational approach is not in the cards. Too many cooks, too little broth, too much noise. Each combination of decision makers and options has its own structure, and each can lead to either good or bad decisions. Some arrangements cannot lead to any decision at all. We'll get to that.

One of our more interesting bits of historical reading is the collection of James Madison's minutes of the Constitutional Convention in 1787. The fifty-five men who assembled there were impressively well educated and informed, head and shoulders above the collective quality of any of our current governing bodies. Yet they had real trouble putting together an effective decision-making system for the new country they were creating. (They weren't sent to Philadelphia to write a constitution, but they did it anyway and got away with it. That was a group decision.) They gave themselves a hard job, creating a form of government that would lead to neither autocracy (they'd had enough of that from the English kings) nor chaos (which they all recognized as worse). The complex system of checks and balances that they devised was meant to steer between these two extremes, while also muting the differences between the small states and the large ones. (We are fortunate that Madison took notes, so we have a good idea of what was said. There were no recording machines.)

Over the past few decades, the needs of the business community have led us to learn a lot about multiplayer (and multicriterion) decision making, and there are conditions in which it is literally impossible to make decisions self-consistently. Who cares? you might say. (Ralph Waldo Emerson wrote, "A foolish consistency is the hobgoblin of little minds." People who misquote this pithy aphorism tend to leave out the key word "foolish," thereby changing the meaning for their own purposes.) The reason to seek self-consistency, in a nutshell, is that if you are not self-consistent, you can get beaten at your own game by an opponent who is. That shouldn't yet be obvious. English bookies call such departures from coherence a Dutch book, for reasons unknown to this author. Of course, in a competitive game with a thinking opponent, a player who is consistent will soon become predictable—an adversary can exploit that for his own benefit. Poker players know this, as do football coaches.

Our deepest social problems (not only in this decade or this century or this millennium or this country or this continent) revolve around finding stable and just ways to govern—to assign decision-making power within a social group, when the decisions made by a few affect all members of the group. The apportionment of benefits, the apportionment of responsibilities, the apportionment of burden, and the apportionment of authority—all need to be faced before one can even speak of government. Among the oldest forms of government are those that involve a leader who, by brute force, by consensus, by age, by birthright, or by the assertion of divine authority, makes decisions binding on everyone. In a stressful situation it is often better to have an acknowledged leader, however incompetent, than to have no leader at all. All armies know that. Absolute authority may not be just, but it works, especially in a crisis. A variant of that system is rule by law (in the broad, and not pejorative, sense), in which there comes into being a rigid and all-encompassing set of rules, provided either by long tradition or by whatever gods may be. This is then searched for guidance on all possible decisions—usually without asking where the rules came from. Various scriptures and the Code of Hammurabi are examples. The Ten Commandments are the short form. Other types of rule involve popular consensus, which drives all decisions toward the lowest common denominator, which may be bad for everyone affected. Still others involve some variant of majority rule (the United States uses a version of that), which may or may not involve some limits on the power of a majority to make decisions that weigh too heavily on the minority. Such limits tend to be eroded by time, and this is inevitable in a popular democracy. (Contrary to almost universal belief, cultivated in the schools, the United States has never declared itself a democracy—the word does not appear in the Constitution or the Declaration of Independence. The Constitution does guarantee to each state a republican form of government, but that has a different meaning, itself not explained in the Constitution.) Winston Churchill's observation that democracy is the worst form of government except for the alternatives neatly summarizes the dilemma. We'll devote a lot of space to this class of problems; the inability of our elected bodies to actually govern has become a matter of widespread frustration and disillusionment in the 1990s. And not just in America. Despite all that, we seem to have embarked on a crusade to persuade everyone in the world, whatever their local circumstances, to adopt some version of our form of government, to say nothing of our economic system. It is not clear to this author just how the decision to embark on this crusade was made, by whom, or how long it will persist. Remember how the original Crusades ended.

When dealing with a complicated subject it is easy to see the forest as a bunch of trees, and to suffocate in the minutiae, while missing the point. A game often contains the essence of the real problem it exemplifies, with minimal mind-cluttering baggage, and can serve as a suitable introduction.

So we'll begin some parts of the book with an educational puzzle that opens up the decision-making issues that lie ahead. Other than that, the book will proceed from the simple to the complicated to the unsolved, from personal decisions when we know the facts, through issues of decision making under uncertainty, through contests, and finally to multiplayer multicriterion decision making, the stuff of governments and big business. It remains to be seen if anyone can invent a form of government that is stable, and actually works, over the thousands of years we read about in science fiction, and see on *Star Trek*. Democracy, in the sense of communal decision making in the common interest, is relatively new on the historical scene, and has yet to pass that test.

Once we have the principles straight, such as they are, there will be some specific examples of decision making at work, ranging from sports, gambling, and investment strategies to some little-known problems, like the apportionment of the House of Representatives—the subject of George Washington's first veto.

Finally, this book is not intended for those who are already expert in statistical decision theory—they have plenty of fine books to choose from. It is intended to help the rest of us to improve our understanding of decision making, to become more inquisitive about *how* decisions are made, both by us and for us, and to function a little more effectively, both as individuals and as citizens.

Why Flip a Coin?

1

Basics:
The First Cut

If we had infallible crystal balls we'd have no trouble making decisions. We'd bet on sure winners, put our winnings into lucrative risk-free investments, share our lives with ideal mates, do a perfect job of raising perfect children in a perfect environment, stay off airplanes and out of cars that are headed for trouble, and lead marvelously rewarding and protected lives. But we don't know all the relevant factors, can't foresee the future, and don't even know now what we'll really want in later life, so we have trouble making decisions. And that's without the extra burden of having several participants in a decision, sometimes working with us, sometimes against us.

When we don't know something—the future, the past, the meaning of life, or our own aspirations—the condition is called uncertainty. It is inescapable, just like death and taxes. The popular view of uncertainty carries images of bumbling, ineptitude, indecisiveness (to which uncertainty may well lead), and weakness, but all the word really means is that there is something we don't know. No shame in that. It may be unknowable, like the future, or it may be easy to find out, like a phone number. Whether or not someone else knows it, if you yourself don't know it, you are harboring uncertainty. Find someone who claims to know everything, and you will have found someone to avoid. This book is about making rational and consistent decisions in the face of uncertainty, which means adjusting to the fact that, while we may not know everything, we always know *something*. And we ought to use what we do know as effectively as we can. Most of the time, anyway.

We will also run into probability, or odds. Most of us know how to use the odds to decide whether to bet on an inside straight in poker, or on a particular team to win the Super Bowl. The problem of decision making is to apply the same principles more widely to the conduct of our lives. We'll come back to uncertainty and probability.

Much of the uncertainty in individual decision making comes from not knowing what we really want to achieve through the decision, and from our tendency to exaggerate both potential losses and potential gains. People buy lottery tickets and play the slot machines at casinos, despite the fact that the casino owners and the lottery managers aren't in business to give away money. For them to make money (and those who don't are soon replaced), the average player must lose money (then it's called a zero-sum game, of which more later). But players still dream of hitting the jackpot. Hopeful gamblers (and the writers of lottery advertising) are fond of pointing out that, after all, *someone* does win. That's exaggeration of potential gain, because it doesn't mean that *you* have a realistic chance of winning. On the other side of the coin, exaggerated fear of harmful effects keeps some parents from immunizing their children against disease, leads them to throw away their electric blankets, and makes them demand that schools root out harmless asbestos in the walls, which would usually have been better left alone. We are terrified of trivial risks, and spend billions in futile efforts to control them. That's exaggeration in the other direction. Both expectations of gain and fears of loss are far too often overblown, to the detriment of balanced decision making.

To make any decision in a rational way, we need to think through the likely consequences of the decision, whichever way we may finally decide to act, and must be honest with ourselves about the importance of the potential gains and losses. (Through all this, we'll assume that the purpose of any decision is to do or to avoid doing something, or to do it differently. Decisions that lead to no action, like a decision to start a diet tomorrow, are no decisions at all. That's why it's so easy to make New Year's resolutions.)

So an individual decision problem consists of a possible set of actions, a possible set of outcomes of those actions, some estimates of how likely each outcome is, given the decision, and some kind of preference ratings for the possible outcomes. Those are the bare bones of the problem, and all that remains is to put some flesh on the skeleton.

We start with a game.

2

The Dating Game

Not only is a game a good way to start learning a subject, there is no real harm in losing. This author, a pilot most of his life, once had the opportunity to fly a DC-10 simulator at the factory. (It was a wondrous gadget, just like the cockpit of the real airplane, swiveling and bouncing realistically, with spectacular scenery passing by in the fake windshield, but still firmly attached to the floor.) He crashed ignominiously, having lost considerable face and reputation, but walked away without a scratch. If you feel an irresistible urge to crash a DC-10, that's the way to get it off your chest. You can lose millions at Monopoly, while learning to be a real-estate wheeler and dealer, and wake up solvent. The game of go is played with devotion throughout East Asia, especially in China and Japan (it originated in China four thousand years ago), even though it is virtually unknown in the United States. It reduces to bare essentials on a simple playing board the most basic strategies of war, and can be played without any damage to people or things (except to the egos of most Westerners who play). It is no accident that chess has kings, queens, knights, bishops, and pawns. An arcade game about tank battles was adopted by the Army as a primary training tool for future tank drivers. And so forth. Never underestimate the importance of games as introductions to life.

The first step in a book on decisions is to convince the reader that there really are ways to make decisions rationally, and that it can make a difference. The second step, of course, is to say how. Most of us will insist that we make important decisions only after "thinking it over," but who knows what that means? When pressed we usually admit that every now and then we simply "take a chance." Sometimes there really isn't much choice, karma and all that, and then we just go along for the ride. A Hobson's choice (named after an English stablekeeper) is a choice that is no choice at all—like Henry Ford's famous comment that a customer can have any color car he wants, as long as it's black. But sometimes the choice is important, the stakes are higher, and straight thinking *can* make a difference. Then it pays to do things right.

So here's our first puzzle, about individual decision making. The problem we've chosen is well known to mathematicians, has an obvious analog in real life, and is interesting in its own right. We make no apology for the fact that it is framed in the context of courtship—that's where many of us make our most important personal decisions, and where we can use all the help we can get. On the other hand, games shouldn't be taken too literally as lessons in life—they are pale shadows of the human condition. This particular puzzle has many other names.

The Dating Game

Imagine yourself a female who has decided, for reasons we cannot possibly explain, to get married (no gender bias intended, exchange the sexes throughout if you prefer—the game's the same), and of course you want to marry the most desirable male from the pool of, say, a hundred eligible and available bachelors in your social circle. Second best simply won't do for a person of your outstanding quality and refinement, let alone aspirations. But finding the best of the lot out of a hundred possibilities isn't going to be easy; you need a strategy.

Obviously, you shouldn't marry the first guy you meet. The chance that he's really tops in the group of a hundred is, of course, a chance in a hundred. That's a pretty slim chance, and a gamble in the worst sense of the word. But the same is true of the second, and the third, and so forth. Any one of those has only a chance in a hundred of being the best of the lot. You can't just pick one at random if you want a realistic shot at the very best. It's like picking the best apple in a barrel—you'd better start comparing them with each other. Any of them can be the best, but it can also be the worst.

So you'll have to do some dating—how else can you check them out against each other?—but the rules of the game are not like those of the apple barrel. In that case you could look at the apples side by side, but in this game you are only allowed one date with each candidate. After each date you have to decide on the spot if this one looks like the very best, even when there are some you haven't yet dated. (They are all eager to marry you— it's a game—so it's your choice.) Once you select the lucky man, you stop dating—games don't have to be entirely realistic. Another rule of the game is that if, after a date, you decide against a candidate, he is lost to you forever. Imagine that he marries someone else, enters a monastery, or hurls himself off a cliff. The point is that you can't date them all in turn, put each one on a shelf in a warehouse after the date, presumably with a rating label, and then later dust off the best. No stockpiling of candidates. Statisticians call this process sequential decision making—you decide on the spot, while you are still collecting information.

This sort of thing happens all the time in clinical trials or drug testing, in which one group of patients is given a potentially useful drug, and another group something harmless but ineffective—a placebo. The people running the tests should be ready to decide at any moment to end the trial, giving the control group the drug (if it's turning out to be useful) or taking the treated group off the drug (if it seems harmful). They shouldn't go on testing any longer than it takes to decide. You shouldn't either, unless you enjoy the dates more than the prospect of marriage— that's another subject.

The selection problem is obvious. You want the best spouse, but how can you maximize your chance of finding him under these rules? If you plunge too early in your dating career, there may be finer, undated fish in the sea, and you may go through life regretting a hasty marriage. It happens more often than we like in real life—marry in haste and repent at leisure, says the old proverb. Yet if you wait too long the best may have slipped through your fingers, and it is then too late. That also happens all too often in real life. Songs, poems, and novels have been written about both misfortunes.

So what is a winning strategy—one that gives you the best chance of success? You can't be sure, you just want the best chance. This is a simple game; you know what you want, everything is in the open, you alone make the fateful decision, and you have only to optimize your selection process. Is there a best way?

You bet there is. It doesn't give you a sure thing, but it does give you the best shot at your goal. No matter how well you organize your affairs to hit the jackpot, there is always a certain risk that you'll simply have bad luck, and end up with the bottom of the barrel. After all, someone does. So let's go through the reasoning.

As we said, you shouldn't choose the first applicant who comes along—it would really be an amazing coincidence (a chance in a hundred) if the best of the lot showed up first. So it would make sense to use the first group of dates, say ten of them, as samplers (as in a candy shop or bakery), and then marry the next date who rates higher than any of those. That's a way of comparing them, and is not far from real life. You could give each date a grade in your diary (say on a scale of ten), and resolve that the first one who comes along with a higher grade than anyone in those first ten is the final winner. All you're doing is using the first ten dates to gain experience, and to rate the field. That's what dating is all about.

There are two ways you can lose badly that way. If the first ten just happen to be the worst of the lot—luck of the draw—and the next one just happens to be the eleventh from the bottom, you will end up with a pretty bad choice—not the worst, but pretty bad—without ever coming close to the best. You have picked the eleventh from the bottom because he is better than any of the first ten—that's your method—while the best is still out there waiting for your call. But at this early stage in your dating career you have no way of knowing that. It's somewhat like running around with a flaky crowd: the experience distorts your impression of what real people are like. The other way you can lose is the opposite: by pure chance the best choice may have actually been in the first ten, leading you to set an impossibly high standard after your early dating experience. You will then end up going through the remaining ninety candidates without ever seeing his equal, and will have to settle for the hundredth because the pool has dried up. The hundredth will be, on the average, just average. You are then doomed to go through life fantasizing about what might have been—the one who got away. So you have a chance of winning, but also a chance of losing big. It's not hard to show (but the mathematics involved is beyond the ambitions of this book) that you have about a chance in four of winning (marrying the best of the lot) with this strategy. Better than a random choice, but not a sure thing. The rest of the time you'll have to settle for second best, or third best, or fiftieth best, or whatever comes up.

Can you do better than that? Well, the chance of the second kind of error, letting the best slip through your fingers, is pretty small for this case—if you've sampled ten candidates out of a hundred, there's only a chance in ten that the best is in that lot. So you might be willing to do a bit more sampling without too much risk of an error of this kind, and thereby improve your knowledge of what's available. You'd get more experience. What about using exactly the same strategy, but going on twenty dates before making your choice? You'll increase the chance that the best candidate slips through your fingers from one in ten to one in five before you are ready for marriage, but will have greatly decreased the chance that you have set too low a standard. It's a trade-off, better in one way, and worse in another. What about thirty dates, or forty? If you go too far you'll almost certainly miss the boat, so there must be a best choice of sample size somewhere in there.

It turns out that the best strategy in your quest for the top of the heap is just this date-rate-and-wait procedure, coolly letting exactly thirty-six suitors go by before selecting the next one who is better than any of those. You still run a risk (about a chance in three) that you've let the best get away, but you've done the best you can do, and actually have about a chance in three of ending up with the one in a hundred you were seeking. A chance in three isn't bad, when you're seeking one in a hundred. (Incidentally, we're not being exact when we say a chance in three. There is an exact answer, but going for six decimal places of precision makes no sense at all for this kind of real-life decision.) If you were interviewing applicants for a job, the same logic would work.

But wait, let's stop for a moment to look at some of the other factors we've downplayed. Are you that sure of your own motivation and ambitions? Do you really and truly *require* the very very best out of the hundred eager swains?

There is a downside of always aiming for the top. If the best candidate was in the first group, you'll end up having to marry the last date of the hundred, the bottom of the barrel but not necessarily the worst of the lot. For this game he would be average, but in the real world he may not be even that good—others are fishing, too. You are betting on a chance in three of getting the best, against about the same chance of settling for an average Joe, or worse. Like always trying for an ace in tennis.

So let's go back to the case in which you were only allowing ten dates to set the standard, and look at it a bit more closely. What has happened is that the top prospect has only a chance in ten of having been in that first group, so he's probably still out there in the big pool of the ninety you haven't yet dated. The only reason he isn't sure to end up with you is that there is just as good a chance that number two is also out there, and it is even money that you'll find him before you date the finest. Either one is better than the first ten, so according to the rules, you'll pick whichever comes along first. In fact, there is the same chance that number three is still there, and so forth. So what is happening is that by having so few premarital dates you've reduced your chance of passing up the top prospect, but in return have increased your chance of missing him for one of the runners-up. But is that so bad? Well, it depends on whether you think you'd be miserable with second best, out of a pool of a hundred. Seems pretty arrogant, doesn't it.

Maybe it would be better to play the game a little more conservatively. Same rules but different objective. Don't insist on maximizing your chance at the first prize, but try to avoid having to scrape the bottom of the barrel. That's called risk avoidance. If you were gambling (and you are, but not for the usual stakes) you might be trying to cut your losses rather than always going for the long-shot high-payoff winner. You would be betting to place or to show at the races, for a bit more security. How would your strategy change?

Once you've decided that, after all, the second best in a crowd of a hundred suitors is really not likely to be too bad, you don't have to go all the way from thirty-six down to ten dates to enjoy the benefits of your more relaxed approach. It turns out that then it's better to let only thirty potential mates go by, and, as before, pick the next who is better than any of those. Though the chance of getting the best decreases a bit, you'll have a better than 50% chance of choosing *either* the best of the lot *or* the second best. And you've greatly reduced the chance of going through your dating career without a decision until the final, last gasp. That makes a lot of sense.

You can carry this further. If you'll settle for any of the top five in the pool, it turns out that you should sample only twenty dates; then you have about a 70% chance of landing one of the top five. Imagine, nearly three-to-one odds in favor of marrying one of the top five candidates in a pool of a hundred suitors, just by using your head. In fact, this more conservative strategy doesn't reduce your chance of getting the cream of the crop all that much; it goes down from about 37% to 33%, which is hardly noticeable. You've greatly improved your average performance, *and* you've cut the chance of running out of suitors nearly in half, just by giving up a wee bit of your chance at the grand prize. But be careful not to go too far; if you push this to the extreme you'll be back to marrying the first guy you date.

There are many different possible strategies for this game, and the optimal one for you—the rule through which you ought to make your own personal decision—depends entirely on how well you can specify your objectives. You can gamble for the best—the first strategy—and accept the chance of losing badly. Or you can relax your criteria a little bit, to cut your losses if that doesn't work out. You have to know, and be ready to declare in advance, what it is you are looking for. For every set of objectives, clearly recognized and stated, there is an optimal strategy of the date-rate-and-wait variety. That shouldn't be a surprise—people do it in real life. You can't have everything—sorry about that—so you'd better be realistic about your goals. (Schoolteachers and preachers may tell you to always aim for the top, but that's a bad strategy for anything important. The better is the worst enemy of the plenty good enough.) You might in fact adjust your goals as you learn more, either raising or lowering your standards as you gain experience, or as the supply runs out. Most people do that instinctively—it's called a dynamic strategy. If you can say what you really want, there is a best way to get there. On the average, of course—nothing is certain. It may have been Damon Runyon who said, "The race isn't always to the swift—but that's the way to bet."

3

Probability

So the road to a decision involves five steps, each simple enough: list the actions you can take (a decision is just a choice among possible actions, including the action of taking no action at all); list the reasonably conceivable consequences of each of the various actions, as best you can guess them; assess, as best you can, the chance (or odds, or probability) that any particular consequence will follow from any particular action (this is an issue we need to get into—the one most people gloss over); find a way to express your objectives, how much you wish for (or dread) the various possible consequences; and finally put it all together in such a way that it can lead to a rational decision. We'll go through the last three of these one at a time, skipping the first two for the moment—they are different for each situation. If you have problems listing either your options or the possible outcomes, your first step is to solve those problems, and there is nothing we can do to help. After all, a decision is a choice *among* options, and its purpose is to optimize the outcome of those actions; if you can't state them, you surely can't choose among them. Of course, there are times in life (and in Kafka novels) when the options are unknown, and cases in which there are completely unexpected consequences, but those real-life tragedies (or delightful surprises) aren't the subject of the book. This chapter sets the tone for item number three, the odds.

People seem to flinch at the word *probability*—it has too many syllables. Besides, it sounds mathematical, and it's become politically correct in our country to be proud of not knowing any mathematics. (We're already paying the price for that.) Yet the same people who shrink at the word *probability* gamble by the millions (both people and dollars), checking the odds on the tote board or in the newspapers, and placing their bets accordingly. They don't even blink when the weather bureau reports a 25% chance of rain, though that's a probability. Probability and odds are versions of the same concept, and we shouldn't dump a useful idea just because mathematicians happen to call it by a big word that carries a lot of freight. There is no difference whatever between a 25% chance of rain and a 0.25 probability of rain, or even three-to-one odds against rain—they are different ways of saying the same thing.

This is not to say that the concept of probability isn't subtle when you dig into its deeper meaning, or that the methods used by mathematicians (and weather forecasters) to calculate it can't be forbiddingly mathematical, but only that the *use* of probability in most decision making doesn't require that kind of fluency. There are lots of occasions in life in which we use things successfully even when we don't fully understand how they work. Most people who use computers in their work or play these days know very little about how the programs they use were written, less about how the computer they are using was designed, and even less about how the internal components of the computer—the central processing unit, for example—function. That doesn't keep them from using their computers productively, most of the time. The same is true of drivers of cars, watchers of television, pilots of airplanes, and generally users of modern technology. You don't have to know how it works in order to use it.

That was not a pitch in defense of ignorance—on the contrary, the more you know about the world you live in, the richer and more satisfying your life will be, and the more effective you will be at everything you do. Someone once said that he had made many mistakes in life, but never because he knew too much. But you don't have to know *everything* before you do *anything;* if you feel that way, you are doomed to paralysis and irrelevancy. A probability is no more than an ordinary fraction between zero and one, a measure of the likelihood that something will happen; a value of zero means it surely won't, and a value of one means it surely will. Everything else is between those two extremes, and a toss-up means a probability of 0.5. (Named, of course, after a coin toss.) If it sounds a bit circular, that's because it is; who ever said what likelihood means? There are deep issues here, if we bite.

And it's an interesting and important subject in its own right, so before we get down to the business of decision making, let's nibble. What do we mean when we say that the odds of an honest coin landing heads up are even money, 50-50, a 50% chance, or a probability of 0.5, all meaning exactly the same thing? It looks like a classic case of circular reasoning, because if the coin came down heads too often for our taste we'd say that it wasn't an honest coin. Gamblers in Western movies (usually in black hats) tend to get blown away from the table if the cards they or their friends are dealt seem to be defying the laws of probability; the characters in those movies must have a pretty good idea of what to expect from a fair deal. And that's it in a nutshell: if a reasonable person has a pretty good idea of what to expect, that is a probability. Believe it or not, that's it! In fact, all it takes to turn that idea into a number is to ask what odds he'd offer in a bet, and then translate those odds into a probability. For a coin, he'd probably say even money, and you'd say, "Aha, that's a probability of 0.5. Put down a buck to win a buck." For a pair of dice you might ask for the odds on a seven, and an educated gambler would say five to one against, leading you to conclude that the probability was $\frac{1}{6}$ or 0.1667. That number may have come from a calculation, or from long experience—it doesn't matter.

Some old-fashioned statisticians or mathematicians will tell you (with great passion) that this is complete nonsense, that the probability is really a measure of what fraction of the time, *in the long run,* the coin will come up heads. If it happens half the time, the probability is 0.5. But which comes first, the chicken or the egg? (Samuel Butler, the author of *Erewhon,* said that a hen is only an egg's way of making a new egg.) Does the coin come up heads half the time, in the long run, because the probability is 0.5, or is that the *definition* of probability? Besides, who's going to stick around for the long run? Who even cares about the long run if he has to place a bet today? And if someone pulls a coin out of his pocket, or the officials in a football game toss a coin for the kickoff, that's a coin that may never have been tossed before. So what kind of fiction is the "long run"? Frequency in the long run is one of the old and outmoded definitions of probability, and it is on the way out among educated statisticians for at least one simple reason: you can state the probability with some assurance *before* you have tossed the coin once, let alone a zillion times. As a matter of principle, you shouldn't base a definition on the results of a test that will never be performed.

This is a deeper issue than we've made it appear to be, and is the focal point for the fervent combat between the so-called Bayesian and frequentist schools of statistics. (The latter is what we've maliciously characterized as old-fashioned.) The frequentists will defend the how-often-in-the-long-run definition of probability, while the Bayesians are loyal to the ask-an-expert definition, yet both will give the same answer for a coin toss. This is an oversimplification of the issue, but there is a real difference in the two philosophies, and we'll see that the difference is relevant to decision making. Decision making is almost always a one-shot deal, and is best done from a Bayesian perspective. (Thomas Bayes, the first to explicitly describe the discipline named after him, was an eighteenth-century English cleric. His work was published posthumously.)

But first, why do both groups give the same answer for a coin toss, before either has tossed a single coin? Because they both know that a coin has only two ways to land, heads or tails (forget standing on edge—obedient coins don't do that), and they both believe, rightly or wrongly, that there is no preference for one face over the other, so they both know that each possible outcome must have a probability of 0.5. That's the only way they can be equal, and add up to one. The same reasoning applies to dice, which have six faces, and would apply to a regular dodecahedron (one of the five possible fully symmetric solid shapes, this one with twelve identical faces) if you had one handy. If the alternatives are really all the same, and they add up to a certainty (a probability of 1.0), all you need do is divide to find the individual probabilities. No one disagrees with that, whatever his or her favorite definition of probability.

But you can get into trouble if you're careless about this kind of reasoning—it is correct only if there is real symmetry among the alternatives. It comes as a surprise to most people that an ordinary U.S. cent spun on a smooth table is more likely to come down tails than heads. There is a real difference in the weight distributions on the two faces of a cent—one is Lincoln's head and shoulders, the other is the Lincoln Memorial—and the difference matters while the coin is spinning. And sports fans can appreciate the illogic of the famous football coach Woody Hayes, who long ago declared his contempt for the forward pass, saying that there are three possible outcomes of a forward pass, and two of them are bad. He was implying, and was dead wrong, that each outcome has the same probability as the others, 0.333 in this case. That's way out of line, as he knew perfectly well. A good professional quarterback will complete about 60 percent of his passes, with interceptions only a few percent of the time. Completions, incompletions, and interceptions are far from equal-probability events. With the same faulty logic, if you play the lottery or run for the presidency, the only possible outcomes are that you win or don't win, but they sure don't have equal probabilities. Sorry.

Without symmetry, and without the long-run results, how then can a frequentist deal with the probability that the Green Bay Packers will win the Super Bowl game in the year 2007? You can probably get odds on that from a bookie or from an imaginative insurance company. The frequentist has to tell you that there is no such probability, because it isn't possible to play the same game often enough to measure the fraction of times the Packers will win. In fact, the game will be played only once (barring war, insurrection, a players' strike, or a hit by a large meteorite), and the Packers may not even be playing. (For Wisconsin loyalists like the author that would be a national tragedy, but it *could* happen.) The pure frequentist who refuses to define a probability for such a case is throwing away a major application of probability to real life. Bookies and weather forecasters flourish on this kind of thing, and you can get odds in Las Vegas on the outcome of nearly any one-shot sporting event, or even on the outcome of presidential elections. There is a probability, as declared by expert and informed oddsmakers, even for single events that are truly never to be repeated. It may vary from oddsmaker to oddsmaker, but so what. The ones who do it badly are soon out of business.

So why does all this matter?

Decision making is almost always about single events—even a toss of a coin is a single event, and there is no way to tell from a single toss whether the coin was an honest one. It may come down heads, or it may come down tails, and we base our estimate of the odds entirely on the assumption, naive though it may be, that it is an honest balanced coin. In the dating game of the last chapter, each date with a new suitor is a gamble (as in real life), and you are not going to go through the exercise of a hundred dates a million lifetimes in a row, just to establish the odds, before you begin serious dating. In doing our calculations we assumed that the suitors were randomly selected (interchangeable, to statistical purists), just as it is habitual to assume that the tossed coin is symmetric and randomly tossed. But there are cases that are not so simple, like horse races that are also run just once, in which the probability that a horse will win varies greatly from horse to horse. Analyses of the way races actually come out show that the predictions of experts are pretty accurate—they really are expert, on the average. And the horses are *not* interchangeable. (More about that in our chapter on gambling.) The chance of rain tomorrow is *not* interchangeable with the chance last Tuesday. (It's fashionable to complain about weather forecasters, but nowadays they do a pretty good job.) The distinguished English statistician Dennis Lindley has used a fine example in which the object being tossed was a thumbtack, not a coin. Then there is no symmetry, and all bets are off (literally) for a frequentist statistician.

So what we mean by probability in the decision-making business is a number between zero and one, measuring the likelihood of a particular event, as well as it can be estimated by whatever tricks are handy. If you need to ask an expert, or a mathematician, fine. But get a good one. If you need to guess, that's fine, too. But don't overrate your own skill—that's a common failing. There may be people who know more than you, and can therefore do a better job of predicting the odds. If you can find one to help you out, do so. But steer clear of phoney prophets, like astrologers, palmists, and readers of crystal balls. (We may have lost some readers on that sentence. Polls continue to show that an appalling and disturbing fraction of Americans still believe in that baloney.)

Of course, the probability business isn't quite that free-wheeling. There are certain rules we have to obey in combining probabilities, lest we get into nonsense and self-contradiction. There are only a few such rules, and they come very close to being obvious. For example, the probability that two unrelated events will both happen is gotten by multiplying the two separate probabilities. If a nickel has a chance in two of coming up heads (a probability of 0.5), a dime has the same probability, and we toss them together, then the probability that they *both* come up heads is one in four, or 0.25. There is a similar, slightly more complicated, law for the "or" case, one *or* the other coin turning up heads (0.75, because the alternative, both coming up tails, has a probability of 0.25). But given the probabilities of the individual events, however derived, the laws for combining them must always be obeyed. Otherwise inconsistencies will crop up and confound the entire decision-making process.

So the three basic laws of probability are:

- The probability that two completely independent events *both* occur is the product of the probabilities for each. This also applies to more than two events.

- The probability that at least one of two *mutually exclusive* (they can't both happen) events occurs is the sum of the probabilities for each. If they are not mutually exclusive, like the nickel and the dime, it's a bit more complicated.

- If the circumstances are that *something* is bound to happen, the sum of the probabilities of those independent somethings is one. For example, *some* team will win the World Series (if it's played), so the sum of the probabilities for each of the teams adds up to one. Again, they have to be mutually exclusive—you can't add the probability that the Cincinnati Reds will win to the probability that the National League will win.

We used those laws extensively (though we kept it to ourselves) in analyzing the dating game of the previous chapter, and even though there are only a few laws, the solution of complex probability problems can be difficult. The principles are not. The one form of mathematics you really need to know to master probability is adding fractions or decimals, and you should have learned that in high school, if not sooner.

Just to make sure that is all straight, let's do a simple problem: calculate the probability of getting four of a kind as a pat hand in a draw-poker deal. Just an example—we don't encourage gambling. Of course, if you know the odds better than your competitors do, gamble away with a clear conscience. You are winning through skill, and that's ethical. There was a legal case not too long ago that dealt with the question of whether a video-poker slot machine was a gambling machine or a game of skill—gambling was illegal in that particular state, but games of skill were not. After heated debate and conflicting testimony from eminent statisticians, the court ruled that it was a game of skill, and therefore legal.

Since we'll be working with a dealt hand, there is no skill at all involved, and we are speaking of raw probability. By probability in this case we mean the fraction of all possible hands that will have four of a kind, calculated through an extension of the symmetry arguments used earlier. It can be worked out just by carefully thinking through the motions of dealing. All that is involved is the use of the same old symmetry arguments over and over again, assuming that all possible hands have the same probability. Then the probability will just be the ratio of "good" hands to all hands.

First, ask how many possible different hands we can get in a deal. We'll count the same poker hand as "different" if the cards arrive from the dealer in a different order. It doesn't matter whether or not we keep the order straight, as long as we are consistent, and do the same for the good hands as for the others. We'll end up taking the ratio. (There are 120 different ways in which a specific five-card hand can arrive from the dealer, so each hand can arrive in 120 different orders. We'll just count them all.)

So the first card we receive can be any one of the original fifty-two, the second any of the remaining fifty-one, and so on to the fifth card. The total number of possible hands, including different orders of receipt, is then $52 \times 51 \times 50 \times 49 \times 48$, which adds up to 311,875,200 possible hands. A bit more than one for every man, woman, and child in the United States. So we could give each person an ordered poker hand as an identification, instead of a Social Security number. For a while.

First Card	Second Card	Third Card	Fourth Card	Fifth Card
	different	same as either	same	same
	48	6	2	1
any card		different	same	same
52		48	2	1
	same		same	different
	3		1	48
		same		
		2		
			different	same
			48	1

How many of those hands have four of a kind? Well, let's go through it. The first card can be anything, since four of a kind can start with any card, so we'll give that one fifty-two options. (Follow the diagram from left to right—that's the first line.) The second card can either match the first (say two aces) or be different—three chances of being the same value, and forty-eight of being different. Now we've dealt two cards, and have two different tracks to deal with.

First follow the top track, in which the second card is different from the first. The third then has to match one of those two, otherwise we won't arrive at four of a kind. So there are six options on the third card (three of each), after which the next two cards must follow the leader. Otherwise we won't have four of a kind. So the top track has a total count of fifty-two for the first card, forty-eight for the second, six for the third, two for the fourth (there are two more of the right cards to be collected at this point, and they can come in either order), and one for the last holdout. The total here is then $52 \times 48 \times 6 \times 2 \times 1$, for a total of 29,952 hands.

Next the bottom branch, in which the second card matches the first, so there are still fifty-two options for the first card, but only three for the second. Now the third can be a match for the first two (there are two such cards left, so two options), or different (forty-eight options). If it's different, then the last two cards must match, for two options and one option respectively, as on the end of the top track. If it's the same, then the first three cards match, and the last two must be the one remaining card of the four of a kind, and one stray, in some order. Either way, the number of possibilities is forty-eight. So, adding it all up, we have for the bottom track $52 \times 3 \times 48 \times 2 \times 1$ plus $52 \times 3 \times 2 \times 1 \times 48$ plus $52 \times 3 \times 2 \times 48 \times 1$, for a total of 44,928.

When this is added to the number of possible hands on the top track, we get 74,880 possible "winning" hands, out of a total of 311,875,200, so the probability of being dealt four of a kind as a pat hand is found by dividing; it is 0.00024, just a shade under a chance in 4,000. Not much of a chance, and it doesn't happen very often. Only a straight flush is less probable, with a chance of less than one in 72,000. You could work that out the same way.

We went through that calculation in dreadful detail just to make a point. If you are systematic and careful, and can do simple arithmetic, you can do any probability problem of this kind. It's not hard in principle, just tedious in practice. And it does take practice.

There is one more point to mention about the probability business, and then on with the show. Up to now we've spoken of probability only in the context of the likelihood that something *will* happen, and never in terms of whether something *has* happened. We hear a loud noise in the sky and ask whether it was thunder, the sonic boom of a fast aircraft, a space shuttle landing, or perhaps Superman jumping high mountains. Where this author lives, the first three are about equally common, the fourth has yet to happen. Within our legal system we judge guilt in criminal trials in terms of "reasonable doubt," meaning that we wish to convict only if there is a very low probability that the defendant is actually innocent of the crime of which he is accused. (We can never be absolutely sure, and mistakes are sometimes made—more about that in Chapter 22.) Since we don't know the facts, we work with probability, though under the table. Judges have standard time-tested circumlocutions for telling juries the difference between reasonable doubt and unreasonable conjecture, but they can't really do a good job of it, and don't even agree among themselves. They are trying to deal with probabilities without mentioning the word *probability*, or, Heaven forfend, using mathematical concepts. A body of case law has been built up to substitute for the precise definitions. That will be our last real chapter, before the epilog.

So there is a use of the probability concept to deal with the likelihood that something may have happened in the past, that Attila the Hun weighed exactly 157 pounds on his sixteenth birthday, that Winston Churchill and Greta Garbo shared a common ancestor ten thousand years ago, or that Mars was once inhabited by a now-extinct race of cuddly teddy bears. (Frequentist statisticians go bonkers on that kind of thing.) All those statements are either true or false, in some abstract and useless sense, but since we don't know the facts we must function in the world of uncertainty and probability. Sometimes research can change these retrospective probabilities as we discover evidence—that is what a great deal of research is all about—but the probabilities properly reflect the uncertainties about past facts and events, just as the probabilities we've been speaking about up to now reflect uncertainties about future events. The definition of probability that depends on an average of many tries is useless in describing uncertainties about the past; the past is surely one thing we can't repeat many times, wish though we may. Someone once said that life can only be understood backwards, but unfortunately it must be lived forwards. Probability goes both ways.

4
Gains and Losses

We still have to invent a way to rate the consequences of a decision. If we don't care a fig about the consequences, we don't have a real decision problem (*che sarà sarà*), but if we want to do better than just go along for the ride, we have to be able to say *what* we want, and how badly we want it. And in helpful terms—a bit better than "gee, that would be nice."

There is one thing we ought to put up front—it will be relevant later, especially when we talk about systems of government. Just as we have no real motivation to make good decisions if we don't care how they turn out, other people who don't care about the consequences ought not to be making decisions for the rest of us. Unless you have a real and personal stake in the outcome, there is no compelling incentive to do the job well. That applies to all jobs. This is taken for granted in the small world of individual decision making—if things go wrong, you have only yourself to blame, and you're the one to reap the whirlwind. But we really don't live alone in the world, making our lonely decisions and suffering the lonely consequences. In the larger world, our decisions also affect the welfare of our friends, neighbors, family, and countrymen. When, perhaps by voting, we participate in decisions that don't affect us personally, but do have a major effect on others, there is a real potential for mischief, and the Founding Fathers were well aware of it. It's hard to resist the temptation to vote selfishly, to tax everyone else and to limit everyone else's freedom. And for politicians the lust for reelection can easily overcome concern for the public interest. We'll have more to say about these issues in the proper context later. For now, let's assume that you have personal reasons to care about the consequences of the decisions you make.

This subject has a long history, and the same ideas can have completely different names, according to the profession of the speaker or writer. We've used an unpretentious title for the chapter, though statisticians and economists sometimes speak of the utility or the loss function, a way of measuring how much you want or don't want a particular outcome. If you want it, you seek to maximize the function, and call it utility; if you don't want it, you seek to minimize it, and call it a loss function. Both reflect the same decision-making problem, and both require the same work, but one is concerned with how full the cup may be, and the other with how empty. This author is neither a statistician nor an economist, so it won't matter. A loss can be considered a negative gain, and vice versa. No harm will be done either way. The half-empty cup quenches just as much or little thirst as the half-full one. And there is nothing sinful about the use of negative numbers.

Utility is simply a sharpening of the idea of gain, to take into account preferences. There are simple cases in which the gain from a decision can be measured directly in, say, dollars; then the purpose of a decision might be to maximize the probable net profit. Many business executives, stockholders, investors, and boards of directors believe that it is engraved in ancestral stone that their *only* objective in life is to maximize the net profit. For them it is the bottom line—the totality of all the gains and losses of the year, large and small—that is finally displayed in the balance sheet that is sent to the stockholders, and which can lead to the firing or promotion of the executives. Or to bonuses. It is said that if you lose only a little bit on each item, you can't make it up on volume, so you must take care of the pennies. Corporate executives (at least the survivors) know that—some governments act as if *only* the pennies matter. (Our Congress passes the federal budget at a rate of well over $10 million a minute, but will argue endlessly about thousand-dollar items.) Mass merchandising empires have been built on tiny profits on individual items. The supermarket business works with gross margins in the range of a few percent, while the yacht business is very different. Sometimes the value of a consequence can honestly be described as the total net gain, and then this particular part of the decision-making job is easy.

But not always. For most of us, the pleasure of winning ten thousand dollars wouldn't be close to the pain of losing ten thousand dollars. We might be tempted to make an even-money bet for ten dollars, win or lose, double or nothing, but not for a thousand dollars. (Make it a million if you're rich, to make the same point.) A recent poll conducted by an investment advisory company revealed that fewer than 30 percent of the respondents would take an even-money bet that would gain them a thousand dollars if they won, but lose five hundred if they lost. Anyone interested in the bottom line would be crazy to turn down an offer like that. This author would accept that one any day of the week, and twice on Tuesdays. It's like flipping a coin for a prize, and having your opponent always contribute two-thirds of the pot. A Las Vegas casino that offered such odds wouldn't last a day. The results of the investment poll are probably as much due to plain ignorance, supported by our national aversion to mathematics, as to investment philosophy, but they also suggest that fear of loss is a stronger motivation for most of us than is the prospect of gain. There's plenty of other evidence of that. Besides, the desirability of money depends on how much we already have. A simple gift of a thousand dollars to this author would generate more happiness than the same gift to Bill Gates, allegedly the richest person in the country. Since decisions are usually made not just to generate wealth for its own sake, but to generate psychological rewards, we have to take that into account in rating the outcome of a decision. There is a marvelous word used by economists to describe this state of affairs: *ophelimity,* which is taken from the Greek, and means the power to give satisfaction.

So a subject called utility theory has been developed over the last few hundred years, to account for the fact that there is more to the consequences of an action than you can learn by just blindly adding up the gains and losses. We saw that already in the second chapter, where we never asked how *much* more desirable it was to choose the cream of the crop as a potential mate— we simply tried a few variations on the ratings, played with the idea of second best, or one of the top five, and let it go at that. What we never did, and it will come up later when we talk about democracy, was address the internal contradictions of real rating systems. A male seeking a mate (we have to equalize the sexes) might prefer Alice to Beatrice, and Beatrice to Celeste, but then perversely prefer Celeste to Alice. There is nothing at all unusual in such real-life dilemmas (that situation is called intransitivity), and they are dilemmas indeed. Imagine doing the puzzle of Chapter 2 if the preferences were all garbled and inconsistent like that.

So for virtually all of the situations we'll discuss for individual decision making, we'll assume there is some kind of self-consistent (i.e., transitive) ordering of the decision maker's preferences among the possible alternatives, and that our job is to make it sufficiently explicit to serve its purpose.

There are cases in which the pros and cons of a given decision may be from different worlds. We all get junk mail that says that we may already have won a million dollars—just send in the coupon to find out. The positive side is the small chance (small indeed) of actually winning something; the negative is the nuisance of sending in the coupon, and the inevitable later flood of even more junk mail from the folks to whom your name and address have doubtless been sold—the sucker list. How are such comparisons to be made? You can't just add up gains and losses on your hand calculator—there is more than money involved. Sometimes, of course, folk sayings are adequate to save a lot of decision-making bother; in this case it is said that if something sounds too good to be true, it probably is.

The utility of a happening—for us a possible consequence of a decision—is a measure of its value, however we choose to measure it. Consider the folks polled by the investment company, who wouldn't risk an even-money possible loss of five hundred dollars against a possible gain of a thousand dollars. Assuming they are rational, they are saying that lost money is twice as valuable to them as gained money. (For folks on fixed incomes, that's not unusual—extra money may buy luxuries, while lost money costs necessities.) But suppose the question was about a loss of a hundred dollars against a possible gain of a thousand—more people would be likely to swallow their fears and take the chance. With a series of controlled tests or experiments you could probably pin down the fact that for many people lost money is two or three or four times more valuable than gained money; you could then assign different utilities to the potential for gains and losses in decision making. You would simply count losses three or four times as important as comparable gains, whatever the ratio turns out to really be. If it is *you* who are going to make the decision, then it is *you* whose ratio needs to be known. And you should then use the utilities in decision making, not the raw gains and losses. One thing is already clear. If lost money is more valuable to you than gained money, as it seems to be for most people, you shouldn't even gamble regularly at an honest casino. You will lose as often as you win, and the losses will hurt more. Remember the word *regularly*. We'll come back to long shots in the chapter on gambling.

But we still have to deal with cases in which nothing at all countable (like money) is involved. Let's go back to the case of Tom (newly christened), who is trying to come to a rating scheme for his potential soul mates—Alice, Beatrice, and Celeste—and assume that he does in fact prefer them in that order. So his preferences are transitive: Alice is best, Celeste is a last-resort choice, and Beatrice is somewhere in between. (Never mind the reason—everyone knows that there is no accounting for taste in such matters.) All we used in Chapter 2 was the order of preference, but now we want to go a step further, and ask *just where* in the scale Beatrice falls. After all, Tom's willingness to accept second best ought to depend on how much worse that really is than achieving his heart's desire. If Beatrice seems nearly as desirable as Alice he might not feel any urgency to move up his preference chain. If she's nearly as undesirable as Celeste, he might want to take a chance. How can we find out? Since taste isn't countable, there are no scores to add up. What we have to do is dig into Tom's mind about his preferences— he is going to be making the decision, and enjoying or suffering the consequences, and we are just trying to help him do it self-consistently.

This author has been a professor most of his life, and professors often rate students on a scale from zero to ten, perhaps calling a grade of six a bare pass (a subjective call, but a numerical rating allows it to masquerade as a precise measurement). Sometimes we do it with letters, A, B, C, D, F (never an E), and then think of an A as worth the same as a 4.0, a B as a 3.0, etc. There is even a set of words to go with the grades: excellent, good, fair, poor, and failing. The numbers are just surrogates for the qualitative judgments, and have no real numerical significance of their own. But by using numbers we tempt ourselves to do arithmetic with them, something we couldn't do with the equivalent letter grades. We could have rated the students as we do in tennis, giving scores of 40, 30, 15, and love—the process would have been the same. (Adding love improves things in life, but not in tennis.) We then go on to compute an average—the infamous GPA, or grade-point average, based on the zero to four scale. We are then pretending that the numbers have real quantitative meaning. They don't—they are simply inventions—yet the GPA has a major influence on students' lives. In all the years this author has been teaching, he has never once heard anyone—student or professor—question the internal logic of translating subjective judgments into a numerical scale that is then averaged. A student with equal numbers of A and C grades will have the same GPA as one who did solid B work, but wouldn't have if we'd used tennis scoring. Should student fates depend on that?

It's the same with the classification of earthquakes. A Richter magnitude 7.0 earthquake is considered very severe, and indeed it is if you're near the epicenter. The Richter magnitude is based on the logarithm of a very specific reading of a very specific instrument (invented by Charles Richter), and is only loosely and empirically correlated with the energy release and damage potential of the earthquake. (Even the otherwise splendid new *Random House Unabridged Dictionary* has the definition wrong.) A less popular but perhaps more relevant rating system, the Modified Mercalli (MM) scale, is rarely mentioned in the press, partly because it seems less scientific (and probably also because seismologists have learned not to mention it in public). It is based directly on damage, which is what most people really want to know. It uses roman numerals, just like the Super Bowl, and the formal definitions of the Mercalli magnitudes (which run from I, hardly felt, to XII, total destruction) are a bit quaint: at MM VI many people are frightened and run outdoors, and dishes break; at MM VII it's hard to stand, and some weak chimneys break off; at MM IX there is general panic, and so forth. The scale makes no pretense of being quantitative; it is just a listing of the various stages of damage and of experience with human reaction to the event. People don't yet average Richter magnitudes or Modified Mercalli magnitudes, but the day will come.

Grades and Mercalli magnitudes (less so Richter magnitudes) are examples of ordinal systems (putting things in order) whose translation into cardinal numbers (precise values) is entirely arbitrary, so that any further numerical manipulation makes no mathematical sense at all. Besides, who among us can write fractions in roman numerals? Utility theory is an effort to find a way to give ordinal ratings enough quantitative meaning to make some manipulation possible, so they can be used in decision making. Let's see how.

Back to Tom and his courtship dilemma. Imagine that Godzilla shows up in town, sizes up Tom's quandary, and decides to force the issue. (Godzilla hates indecision.) He (or it) tells Tom that he *must* choose Beatrice (recall that Tom's order of preference is Alice, then Beatrice, and finally Celeste) unless he is willing to make a little gamble. The gamble (if he wins) will give him a shot at his favorite, Alice, but with the risk (if he loses) of being left with Celeste. His decision is simple: gamble for the choice between Alice and Celeste, or don't gamble, and go off into the sunset with Beatrice. If Tom chooses to gamble, he'd clearly like to win, and what we want to find out is *how much* he'd prefer Alice to Beatrice, or how strong is his distaste for Celeste, always compared to Beatrice. So the all-powerful visitor, Godzilla, puts it to him straight: settle for Beatrice if you wish, or forget her and flip a coin, even money, for a choice between Alice and Celeste. (Just as in the reverse fantasy of Chapter 2, the candidates are all eager to be chosen.) If Tom says no to the gamble, that implies either that he doesn't consider Alice that much more desirable than Beatrice, or else that he considers Celeste a risk he'd rather not take, at even money. Either way, it gives us information on where Beatrice ranks in Tom's mind between Alice and Celeste, which is the information we are seeking.

Whatever Tom's choice, Godzilla can then try again with a different set of odds, until we eventually come to odds that leave Tom unable to decide whether or not to gamble. We have then found out exactly where he rates Beatrice, on a scale ranging from Celeste up to Alice. In terms of utility theory, if we gave ratings of zero to Celeste and ten to Alice, then if he declines the even-money bet it means that he rates Beatrice as better than a five. If instead he has a low opinion of Beatrice, nearly as low as he has of Celeste, he would jump at an even-money chance to end up with Alice, and would even bet at worse odds. Especially if the worst that can happen, life with Celeste, isn't that much worse than a forced union with Beatrice. By finding the odds at which he is unable to choose (the technical wording is that he is indifferent), we've found a way to rate the Beatrice option against the others. We will have found a scale for his preferences, and it can then be used in decision making.

This way we can build up a rating system, even for things that can't simply be added, by asking at what odds someone is willing to gamble to get a better selection. The worse the odds at which Tom is willing to gamble in his eagerness to avoid Beatrice, the lower his apparent esteem for her. The rating scheme based on such considerations is called the utility, and each consequence of a decision can be given a value for its utility, based entirely on this kind of estimation of its desirability. We would base the utility of winning (or losing) a thousand dollars in terms of the odds the decision maker would be willing to accept in such a bet. As we mentioned, people seem to assign a higher value (negative) to potential losses than to potential gains. So there is a higher (negative) utility for a thousand dollars lost than for a thousand dollars won. It is the utility of a possible outcome that determines its weight in decision making. This is an improvement over simply ranking options in order, as we did in Chapter 2, and will lead to decisions more in keeping with the inner aspirations of the decision maker.

Now we can put these ideas together.

5

Putting It All Together

The point of rational decision making is to help make the best possible decision *on the average.* Over a lifetime you'll end up ahead if you are rational, even if sometimes you turn out to have been dreadfully wrong or surprisingly right. The gurus who flash across the television screens for having correctly guessed the course of the stock market in any given year hardly ever repeat their successes the following year, and with rare exceptions haven't really earned their fame. And gamblers who think they are having a hot night usually learn better before the night is over. Or the next day, or the next week. The laws of probability are mighty powerful, and they never sleep. If this were more widely understood there'd be a lot less crowing about good luck, and a lot less guilt about bad luck. And we'd have a more civilized world. Some things really do happen by chance, and there is little we can do to change that.

Popular books about probability often point out that if you put enough monkeys near enough typewriters for long enough, one of them may just possibly bang out an excellent Shakespearean sonnet. (Actually, there aren't enough molecules in the entire universe to make enough monkeys and typewriters to give this one a fair shake, but who cares? The writers are only trying to make the point that it's not totally absolutely completely impossible.) If, against all odds, it did happen, it wouldn't mean the successful monkey was a reincarnation of Shakespeare, or even literate, but only that the laws of probability are right. Neither monkeys nor humans can take credit for that. (More likely, of course, some prankster faked it.) Underdogs do win football games, all-but-certain winners do lose, and sleepers do win horse races, even when there's no hanky-panky. That's the same as good decisions turning out badly and dumb decisions well—it *can* happen. But not as often as the other way around—favorites win more often than long shots, even in horse races. Remember what Damon Runyon said.

So how do we give decision making our best shot, now that we have the tools? We have to put together the list of possible actions, the possible consequences of each action, the probabilities (expressed somehow, the more carefully the better) that each consequence will follow from each action, and finally we have to put a value on the joy or grief that each of these consequences may bring to you, the decision maker. Then, from all that, we have to find the expected value or utility of each possible action, and choose the best. It sounds complicated, but really isn't, and even trying to go through the process can force us to think. We don't have to do it perfectly to stay ahead of the game. In the real world we don't have to do *anything* perfectly to stay ahead of the game.

When we try to list the consequences that can follow from each of our possible actions, we are thinking of a kind of double list, say a list of possible actions across the top of the page, and under each of those actions a list of possible consequences. Some consequences may be the outcome of several different actions, though with differing probabilities. These can be put down on paper as a sort of double array, what mathematicians call a matrix, with each action and each possible consequence of that action labeled with both the probability and the utility of that particular outcome. Of course the matrix alone would only collect in convenient form what you already know—it wouldn't achieve much simplification of the process, let alone synthesis of the information.

The synthesis shows up through the idea of *expected* utility, or *expected* loss, in which we weight each possible outcome according to its probability—giving it more weight if it is more probable, and less if it doesn't have the ghost of a chance. (You can't fall off a horse if you go for a walk.) All that means is that for every possible decision you should take the value to you of each consequence, multiply by its probability, and add them up. The sum will be the expected utility of that decision, and will tell you how good that decision is for your well-being. The bigger the better.

The importance of introducing the word *expected* is that the actual value to you of any potential benefit (or harm) depends on its probability of actually showing up. If you have an even chance of winning ten dollars, that has an expected value of five dollars—that's what you could sell the chance for. If a lottery ticket has a chance in a million of winning a million dollars for you (forgetting utility for the moment), its expected value is a dollar, and that's what it's worth. People buy stocks at prices that reflect the expected value, both in terms of future earnings and resale value. The idea that you should multiply a probability by a value is nothing new. (We'll see later that that is the best way to understand gambling strategies.) So the expected value of a decision follows the same familiar rules. Let's see how.

Start with one that is simple and familiar, yet has an unexpected twist that has only recently been noticed: the ubiquitous (though doubtless frowned upon by the management) office football pool. In such a pool there is a list of football games to be played on a given day, and a participant in the pool simply buys a chance to guess the winners. The pool proceeds consist of the antes contributed by the players as they buy their chances, and the pot is ultimately shared by the winners. It's simple enough, and you'd think that the best strategy is simply to know more about the teams than the other players. Of course that's true—being smarter or better informed always helps—but there is a little additional trick.

Most pools will let a player buy several entries, so he can "hedge his bets." After all, that brings more money into the pool, which helps it thrive. This means that each player really has two separate decisions to make, the number of entries to buy and the teams to select for each entry. It is still a zero-sum game—all the money put into the pool is delivered to the winners.

For games like a lottery or a horse race (which are not really zero-sum games—the sponsors rake in a bundle), if you buy more than one chance you simply lose money faster. (This is a version of the dictum mentioned earlier, that if you are losing money on the sale of each item, you can't turn a profit by selling more.) But a football pool is an exception—it actually pays to bet against yourself, to buy a second entry. That sounds crazy, and goes against all instinct—how can betting against yourself help? Let's see how it works.

To keep it simple, suppose there is only one game that day, between the Ducks and the Geese, and there are only two participants in the pool, you and Fred. You are equally good at picking winners. Suppose also that the two teams are evenly matched, so the game is a genuine toss-up. Fred buys a chance for two dollars and picks the Ducks to win, then it's your turn. You can pick the Ducks or the Geese, or can get clever. If you buy only one entry, and select the same team as Fred, neither of you can end up ahead. If the Ducks win you are each right, and will split the pot, each getting back two dollars. If the Geese win, you'll still split the pot, since there will be no winner. If, on the other hand, you bet the opposite of Fred, one of you will always collect the winnings, and the other will lose. That's the way to go if you are really better at picking winners than Fred is. But if you are not, and the teams are really equal, you will lose as often as you win. In the long run, you'll both come out even. No road to wealth there.

But what if you buy two chances, betting once on each team? You now have four dollars in the pot, compared to Fred's two dollars, but one of your two tickets will *always* be a winner (and the other *always* a loser). So you will *always* at least share in the winnings. But will you make a net profit?

Well, the game is even money, so half the time the Ducks will win. When that happens you and Fred will each hold one winning ticket, so you will share the six dollars in the pool. You will get three dollars for your four-dollar investment, and will be out a dollar, which Fred will have won.

But what if the Geese win, also an even-money chance? Then you collect the entire investment for yourself, including Fred's contribution, and have won his two dollars for your pains. So half the time you'll win two dollars and the other half you'll lose one dollar—you'll win over the long term. You will net a dollar every two times you play, on the average, for a net expected gain of a half-dollar per pool day, on a four-dollar investment. And without thinking, since you are just betting against yourself. Fred can only win if he's very good at picking winners, picking right two-thirds of the time. (It doesn't matter how good you are, since you're betting both ways.) If there's a pool every week, and he's right only half the time, that's an average rate of return for you of over 12 percent per week, which isn't bad. (Over the course of the year you'll multiply your investment by nearly a factor of five hundred—the magic of compound interest. Fred will, of course, catch on long before then.) It is more complicated and less lucrative with more players and more teams playing more games, but the principle is the same: it pays to hedge your bets.

Now a caution, dear Reader. Please don't rush off to squander money on football pools, using this "system." This whole calculation was based on the assumption that the other player will lose as often as he'll win—that he is, in effect, flipping a coin. If the other player really knows something about the teams, and can pick the winner consistently, this scheme is worthless. It is based on probability, and anyone who can make a good guess about who is *really* going to win can usually beat someone who knows less. Many years ago a professional jockey was asked if he ever bet on horse races. His ingenuous answer was, "Only if I've been told in advance who is scheduled to win." Professional wrestling has the same reputation. The lesson is to avoid games in which the other players know more than you do.

Now let's move on to an example that does a better job of putting the principles together, but is still simple enough to analyze: should you invest your savings in secure bonds or a bank, or go off to gamble at Las Vegas or a suitable surrogate? That will involve a decision, some knowledge of the odds, assessments of alternative outcomes, considerations and ratings of your own objectives, and, finally, trade-offs between instant gratification and respect for the future.

So suppose you have $1,000 in hand, a bank around the corner, and a casino across the street. (You live in a well-serviced neighborhood.) To be even more specific, we'll have the bank offer you 5 percent interest (just about right at the writing of this chapter), while the casino game that attracts you is roulette, where you prefer to play red and black. (For those who are unfamiliar with roulette, there are variations among the wheels, and also in the rules, but a typical American wheel has thirty-eight possible holes, of which eighteen are red and eighteen black, so the chance of the ball landing in a red or a black hole is the same, a bit less than even money. The probability for each is

$^{18}/_{38}$, approximately 0.4737. The odds on winning with either red or black are considerably worse than the odds of 0.4929 for the shooter in a craps game. Craps offers the shooter a much better chance than roulette. More about that in Chapter 19.)

To start you have to have a goal—that's the first and overriding rule of all decision making. If your plan for the gambling option is to play until you go broke, then you will. The small odds in favor of the house will add up over a long enough period of time, and you will surely, eventually, leave the casino a sadder and poorer person. (Whether you are also wiser depends entirely on you.) The only interesting question is how long it takes, and we'll come back to that in a moment.

The bank option is easier to analyze—you lose everything instantly! You will, of course, get a passbook or some other kind of evidence that your money is being held in trust for you, and indeed you can have it back any time you ask (although banks do occasionally go belly-up), but while it is in the bank it is of no use at all to you.

Of course that's misleading. Interest is accumulating, and is being dutifully noted in some record somewhere, perhaps even in your passbook, and you know in your heart that you can always withdraw both the principal and the accumulated interest. That is the trade you have made for giving up the immediate use of your money, and it seems like a good trade when compared to the inevitability of loss in the casino. Many hortatory articles have been written about how interest can accumulate—in a mere century your $1,000 will have built up to nearly $150,000 (compounded daily, as banks with computers now do it). But, you may well ask, what good will that do you?—you won't have much of a chance to enjoy it. The utility of your money decreases as its availability moves further into the future. That's why banks have to pay you interest before they can get their hands on it. (We're ignoring inflation here. Like a rising and falling tide, it just changes the apparent value of all benefits and losses when they are measured in monetary units. It is an illusion, except to people on fixed incomes, or with fixed savings. Of course, the function of inflation in the economic picture is precisely to take money away from such people, to plunder their savings in order to pay for immediate needs, usually for others. There's no other legal way to get something for nothing. Ponder the morality of that, if you will.)

Even so, in terms of long-term prospects the bank is a sure winner over a casino in which you are doomed to go broke. But how long will it take to go broke in a casino, assuming you play to the end? Well, with the rules we've laid down, this is exactly what mathematicians would call a random-walk problem. Imagine a drunk walking near the edge of a cliff—each step he takes has a probability of 0.4737 of moving him away from the cliff edge, and the slightly greater probability of 0.5263 of heading him toward the cliff, so in the long term each step brings him 0.0526 steps (the difference between these two numbers) nearer to the edge. It may take a while, but over he will go. Think of the cliff edge as bankruptcy. If he takes smaller steps (makes smaller bets) it will take longer, but the outcome is never in doubt. About every twenty spins of the wheel, in the casino case, the average loss will be the size of the bet. If a spin takes a minute, you could gamble for sixteen hours before losing your $1,000, on the average, by betting $20 each spin. And somewhere along the way (we'll come to that in a moment) there is even a good chance you'll be temporarily ahead.

That's exactly why you should have specific objectives, decided in advance, and why you should quit when you achieve them, if you ever do. There *is* a chance of quitting while you're ahead, but no chance at all of winning if you stick it out until you're broke. And that's what makes the problem interesting.

So suppose you go into the casino with your $1,000, and are determined to quit when (and if) you double your money. The cry in old-time craps games was "Baby needs a new pair of shoes," meaning, in this case, that you desperately need an additional $1,000 to buy something important. The $1,000 you start with won't do it, but $2,000 will. You recognize that you may lose everything, indeed that you are most likely to do just that, but your need is great. The bank is a loser for short-term needs—it would take nearly fourteen years to double your money at 5 percent interest, and Baby will have outgrown the need for the figurative shoes long before then. So how do you maximize the chance that you will be ahead $1,000 in the casino at some point before you go broke, so you can cash in your chips and quit?

There is, of course, no sure way to win, but you *can* maximize your chance.

That's a well-defined mathematical problem, beyond our scope in this book, so we'll just give the answer. (The drunk-by-the-cliff analogy is still valid: He starts his walk halfway between a bench and the edge of the cliff, and is looking for the best chance to get to the bench before falling off. The bench is the new pair of shoes, or whatever it is that he wants, and the cliff edge, as before, is bankruptcy.) Well, given our rules that you are going to bet $20 per spin, the answer is that you have just about a chance in two hundred of doubling your money before you go broke. That's a mighty slim chance of winning, and a near certainty of losing, making it a terrible decision to visit the casino for the money you need. *Provided* you bet $20 at a time.

You can do better than that, even at the casino. If you bet $50 per spin, everything will go faster and you won't have as much fun, but your chance of quitting with double your money will go up to better than a chance in ten—twenty times as good! Why is that? It simply doesn't take as many strokes of luck to get there, and each one is a challenge to the laws of probability. Sometimes the laws of probability break your way, and that's called luck. Double your bets to $100 at a crack and you're up to a chance in four, which is beginning to get respectable if you really need the money so badly that you are willing to absorb the (still more probable) loss of all of it. By now it's clear where this is going: If you really need the money, and are not gambling for the fun of it, your very best strategy is to put down the whole $1,000 on one spin. It will all be over in a minute, you will have either won or lost, and your chance of winning is only slightly worse than even. Compare that to a chance in two hundred if you make twenty dollar bets! The drunk should close his eyes, point in some direction, and take a giant leap. He has slightly more than an even chance of going over the cliff, compared to a dead certainty if he just wanders around until it happens. But he *could* end up sleeping peacefully on the bench.

If you gamble for entertainment, by all means bet only small amounts. You will almost certainly lose in the end, but it will take a while, and you may conceivably have fun. (Gamblers at casinos don't look as if they're having fun, but that's another matter.) If you gamble in the hope of making a killing, and are in a position to take the loss, bet the farm. Kipling wrote a poem with the lines "If you can make one heap of all your winnings; And risk it on one turn of pitch-and-toss . . ."

But how did we ever come to a conclusion that appears to favor a decision to gamble rather than save, when gambling in the face of the house percentage is a sure-fire bad decision in the long term? What we did was play with the idea of utility.

Recall that in the last chapter we emphasized that the *utility* of money isn't necessarily the same as the *amount* of money. We were actually trying to make the point that, for most people most of the time, it is more painful to lose a certain amount of money than it is gratifying to win it. Such people (i.e., most people) shouldn't even gamble at even-money odds. However, there are times when the need for a certain amount of money (symbolized by Baby's new pair of shoes) makes the chance of winning weigh more heavily than the potential loss. Then the right decision, leaving questions of morality aside, is to gamble, even though there is a net expected loss. Appropriate assessment of the utility of money (or of anything else) can switch a decision around.

It is just this reasoning that drives people to the lotteries, which are increasingly substituting for hated taxes as a source of state income. The fact that they are indeed sources of income for the state is proof enough that they take in more money than they give out, so the citizens (more specifically the players) lose on the average. All mathematicians (beware of all sentences that contain the word *all*—they are usually wrong) will advise against buying lottery tickets. But the public buys them, seemingly oblivious to the certainty of loss, and it's not entirely from ignorance.

A distinguished engineer, a revered friend of the author, gave the reason succinctly in a recent speech. He admitted that he had stopped by a roadside minimarket to buy some essentials on his way home, and had taken his change in state lottery tickets instead of money. The reason, loosely quoted: "Heck, winning a million dollars would change my lifestyle, while losing a couple of dollars won't." He was, in effect, making a declaration about the utility of money, and boosting the utility of winnings relative to losses. To his discredit, however, he was not accounting for the negligible probability of winning in calculating the *expected* utility of a win—that might well have reversed the decision. It may be that most buyers of lottery tickets make the same unconscious assessment, self-justified with the thought that *someone* has to win. Yet there are cases in which this kind of inversion of utility, even when the odds are properly accounted for, can lead to a defensible decision to gamble. This author, however, does not take lottery tickets for change.

So let's end the chapter with a careful statement of the optimal strategy for an individual decision. Call the possible actions *a, b, c,* and so on, and the possible outcomes *A, B, C,* and so on. For each pair there will be a probability, which we can call zero if the action can't possibly lead to the given outcome—for instance, a decision not to get married can't possibly lead to divorce. We also need the utilities, however estimated, of the various outcomes, and we might as well just include them in the *A, B,* and *C.* For decision making all that matters is the utility of an outcome, not its description. Then we have a table like this:

	A = 17	B = 9	C = 15	
a	5	3	7	217
b	4	2	9	221
c	4	6	5	197

We've filled the inside of the matrix with pretty random numbers, to represent the probabilities of the various outcomes for the different actions. (Forget the right-hand column and the top numbers for a moment.) Notice that, unlike real probabilities, we haven't made any effort to keep the numbers between zero and one, because we're just going to compare the different actions, and all that matters is their *relative* ranking. We have, however, been careful to make all the rows add up to the same number horizontally, so no action on the left has an unfair advantage over the others. (If we were dealing with real probabilities this would be automatic. The rows would all add up to one, because the total probability that *something* will happen is one.)

The missing information is still the set of utilities for the possible outcomes *A, B,* and *C,* which will represent our ratings of how badly we want or dread those outcomes. (If we dread them, we can put in negative numbers.) For this example, let's just wildly assume that *A* is worth 17, *B* is worth 9, and *C* is worth 15. That is what is shown on top. We slightly prefer *A* to *C*, and much prefer either to *B*.

Then the expected utility is found by multiplying the pseudo-probabilities by the utilities, and adding across, to get the final numbers on the right. Action *a* yields a return of 217, action *b* gives 221, and action *c* lags with 197. So your best bet turns out to be action *b*, but only by a hair's breadth. It wins despite the fact that it gives a higher probability to *C* than to *A*, though you prefer *A*, but provides an even lower chance of *B*, which is at the bottom of your preference list.

And that's it. You will rarely, if ever, go all the way through this elaborate procedure to make a decision, but if you remember the basic logic, you will make better decisions—in the long run.

6

Stability:
The Social Island

By stability we mean the tendency of any process, in our case the decision-making process, to settle down after a while, and not keep jumping around. We all know people who can't seem to make up their minds about anything, but there are also decision-making situations that *in principle* can't come to a conclusion, regardless of the skill of the decision makers. This chapter is meant to raise the question.

Up to now we've taken it for granted that the systematic procedure for listing actions, consequences, probabilities, and preferences (utilities) will lead us to the best long-run choice. We made it that way by rating all the consequences in terms of their expected utility, so that all that was necessary at the end was to put them in order. When you put things in a line, one of them will be at the head of the line. Since each expected utility has a number assigned to it, and real numbers can always be put in order, optimized decisions then follow easily.

But suppose you have a situation involving the intransitivity we mentioned in Chapter 4. You have gone to your favorite ice-cream store for a cone (you are an addict), have the traditional choice of vanilla, chocolate, or strawberry, and are not such a confirmed and indecisive addict (to say nothing of overweight) that you will order a triple-dipper with one scoop of each. Your self-control limits you to one dip, but you prefer vanilla to chocolate, and chocolate to strawberry. No problem there, unless, when faced with a direct choice between strawberry and vanilla, you'd prefer strawberry. *Then* you'd have a problem. It's not hard to imagine such a situation—it happens because you focus on different features for each comparison. The problem is obvious: whichever flavor you pick, there is one you'd prefer. If the only information available is what we have given, there is in fact no rational or systematic way to choose. The instability becomes embarrassing when you order, say, chocolate, then say, "Shucks, I'd prefer vanilla"; then, looking at the options as the clerk begins to dip the vanilla, "On second thought, I'd really like strawberry," and so on. Eventually you'll be thrown out of the store with no ice cream at all.

Of course, you could handle this the way we've been doing it—force yourself to give a rating or score to each of the three flavors, and pick the highest. There is no way on earth in which you can give vanilla a higher rating than chocolate, then chocolate a higher rating than strawberry, and then turn around and give strawberry a higher rating than vanilla. Ordinary arithmetic won't stand for that. It's only if you have preferences, and can't rate the options in a unique order, that you get into trouble. Then you can have an instability in the decision-making process, and it's not uncommon.

Let's raise the ante, with a case in which there are many decision makers, and their decisions are interlocked. It is also a game, but the players must play according to strict rules, and have no decision-making authority at all. In that sense, it illustrates instability, but not decision making. (The author first saw this example in a series of delightful lectures by Donald Knuth.)

The Social Island

Instead of an unmarried female with a hundred eager suitors, as in Chapter 2, this game involves a collection of married couples (no singletons allowed) living as neighbors on a remote tropical island. Let the first two pairs be called Al and Alice and Bob and Barbara, respectively. We can add pairs alphabetically as we go along. It is all, of course, purely fictitious and contrived, designed to make a point. Ah, but what an island!

The game has unusual, but vaguely familiar, rules. The players have lived together on the island for so long that they know each other very well, and each wife has a secret list of preferences among the husbands, from best to worst, while each husband has his own secret preference list of the wives. It is a world of uninhibited fantasy. Not only that, but the top preference for any given wife may or may not be her own husband, and similarly for the men—that situation is also not unknown in real life. What is to be done about it, other than nurture frustrations? Well, the rules of the game provide an outlet. They stipulate that if, for example, Al really prefers Barbara to his own wife, Alice, *and* Barbara really prefers Al to her own husband, Bob, then Al and Barbara will bid fond farewell to their respective spouses, and wed each other. Since on this special island it is forbidden to be unmarried, there is no option for the jilted pair, Bob and Alice, but to marry each other. That's the full set of rules of the game; now consider some possible cases.

Start with the one we just invented. It can be described by the following table, listing the preferences for each of the four participants:

Al	Alice	Bob	Barbara
Barbara	Al	Barbara	Al
Alice	Bob	Alice	Bob

where the column under each name is that person's preference list. We have been lazy in setting this up, and have chosen to let each person have the same preference list as the other of the same sex; Al and Barbara are everyone's favorites, and Bob and Alice are in everyone's doghouse. That's again not unusual in real life—someone may be everyone's favorite female, and someone else everyone's favorite male. (Blame it on television.) On this island, the wishes of the losers are irrelevant to what happens next. After the trade in which Al and Barbara tie the knot, leaving Bob and Alice to console each other, the table will look like this:

Al	Barbara	Bob	Alice
Barbara	Al	Barbara	Al
Alice	Bob	Alice	Bob

and we see that there will be no further changes. Al and Barbara are happy together, so the fact that Bob and Alice have been mistreated doesn't matter. (Remember, it's a game.) Though Bob and Alice would each prefer a different spouse, Al and Barbara have no further interest in trading, and it takes two to tango. At least on this island. The situation has become stable, and it is possible to prove that a two-couple group will always achieve stability through this process. This doesn't mean everyone is happy, but it can only change if some *couple* agrees, both members, to dump their respective spouses. Again, just like real life. Notice that there were two people living with their preferred mates before the trade, and a different two after, so it can be argued that no net social good has come of this—or harm, for that matter. What happiness there is in this little society has simply clustered into one family. For those who prefer a stable society above all, this is one.

But what if there are more than two couples, say three or four or dozens? Then there are far more possibilities for the preference tables and for the arrangement of marriages, and anyone can play with the various options. (One can see this developing into a party game, with real people making up their own secret lists. But it could never catch on—think of how ego-bruising it would be to have your spouse reveal his or her preference list at a party, with your own name near the bottom.) The result of careful analysis—which can be checked by trying a few cases—is that, whatever the number, and regardless of the preference lists, there is always *some* stable arrangement, but it is no longer true that you can always get there through spouse trading. Consider the case of three couples, with the preference table shown (we've added Charlie and Carol to our small world, and have been a bit sneakier about setting it all up).

Al	Alice	Bob	Barbara	Charlie	Carol
Barbara	Al	Barbara	Charlie	Alice	Bob
Alice	Charlie	Alice	Al	Barbara	Charlie
Carol	Bob	Carol	Bob	Carol	Al

If we then follow the sequence of events, we'll see that Barbara will join Al (she prefers him to Bob, and Al prefers her to Alice), then she'll continue her climb to Charlie (who prefers her to Carol, while he is her first choice). By then Alice has been saddled with Bob, her last choice, so she will move to Charlie, a step up, since he thinks she is really tops, and finally back to Al, her favorite. In every case, the philandering male is also improving his own position.

But now we see the problem: all these shenanigans leave us back exactly where we started, so the cycle can begin again, and go on forever. Even though there are stable marriage arrangements for this crowd (find them if you must), there is no way to get there from the starting point we chose. It is an unstable society.

It is possible to prove that there are always stable arrangements, whatever the preferences and whatever the number of couples (see the next paragraph for examples), but that it is not always possible to get to one of them from a particular starting point. Besides, the stable arrangements may have little to commend them other than stability. Yet in every case of a trade the total amount of happiness in the society stays the same—it is just redistributed among the families.

Take an extreme case in which (for any number of married couples) each man is married to the woman at the very top of his preference list. That is a stable arrangement, because no man will be interested in trading—he is happy to leave things as they are. We could even have each of these men at the bottom of his wife's preference list—it would still be stable because she can't find an unhappy man who prefers her. (Don't ask how it ever happened—tastes change.) And the rules of the game, just as in real life, require agreement between the two elopers. So it is stable, but not necessarily desirable. The gender-reversed case is also, of course, stable, with happy women and unhappy men. And there are many stable cases in between, along with many that will never achieve stability.

We'll leave it at that. The game can be played more ferociously, with dating, engagements, and such amenities, and the general conclusion is what free societies learned long ago: that the more opportunities people get to exercise and explore their preference lists, the better the chance that the final marriage arrangements will be stable. This is, of course, such a contrived game that that particular conclusion shouldn't be taken too seriously, but one should take seriously the central fact that when you have a large group of people, with conflicting aims, stability is not guaranteed. That will come through as a major issue when we talk about social choices later.

7

The Prisoners'
Dilemma

We begin the excursion into multiparty decision problems with a famous classic, the so-called Prisoners' Dilemma, just to get it into the book, and to show that there are deceptively simple decision problems that don't have elegant solutions. It will be the first example in which the best decision for an individual player can depend on what he knows or can guess about another player's intentions.

Jerry and Keith are arrested on suspicion of having committed some awful crime, and are held incommunicado in separate cells. The police and prosecutors are quite certain they're guilty, but aren't sure they can prove it to a jury. (Perhaps convincing evidence was found during an illegal search, or through illegal wiretapping, and can't be used in court. Or they blurted out confessions before being "Mirandized." Or a key witness has mysteriously disappeared.) So without being allowed to communicate with each other, each is separately offered a deal: Keep claiming your innocence in court, while we all know you are guilty as sin, and we'll prosecute you for some lesser crime, which we know we can prove, getting you each two years in jail. That's a sure thing if you're both noncooperative. We'll be really annoyed that we can't pin the real crime on you, but we'll punish you as much as we can, even if it's only two years in the jug.

If, on the other hand, you both confess and repent, you'll get five years each, which is pretty lenient for such a terrible crime, but more in keeping with its seriousness than two years would be.

However, and here's the deal, if one of you confesses and testifies for the state, while the other keeps insisting on his innocence, the one who confesses will get off with just thirty days—after all, we'll appreciate the cooperation, but can't just turn you loose—while we'll throw the book at the unrepentant holdout, getting him ten years in jail. That's the deal, take it or leave it.

The prisoners can't consult each other, yet each one's fate depends on a decision by the other. Consider Jerry's position first. If they stick together, both proclaiming innocence, they'll go to jail for two years, which is a lot better than five. But that depends on both of them—if that no-good Keith confesses, and Jerry doesn't, then Jerry will go to jail for ten years, while Keith gets off almost scot-free. So maybe Jerry should confess—he'll get thirty days if Keith holds his ground, but five years if Keith also confesses. That would be worse than the two years if they both hold firm, but better than the ten years if Keith betrays him. So the bottom line for Jerry is that if he confesses, he'll get thirty days or five years, depending on what Keith does, but if he keeps mum the options are two years or ten years, again depending on Keith. What to do?

Here's the table, where the numbers are Jerry's and Keith's jail terms, in that order.

		Jerry	
		confess	deny
Keith	confess	5 years, 5 years	10 years, 30 days
	deny	30 days, 10 years	2 years, 2 years

Having read a book on decision making, Jerry makes up the table and stares at it, and it suddenly hits him between the eyes that his best decision doesn't depend at all on what Keith does. If Keith confesses, Jerry will get five years if he also confesses, but ten years if he doesn't. If Keith doesn't confess, then Jerry will get thirty days if he does confess, and two years if he doesn't. So regardless of what Keith does, Jerry's best strategy is to confess.

The trouble here is that that's exactly what Keith is thinking, so *his* best strategy, regardless of what Jerry does, is also to confess.

But where does this leave us? Each of the prisoners has made a careful analysis of all the options open to him, and has decided that his best choice, *in his own best interest,* is to confess, regardless of what the other does. They will each get five years in jail in what would be called a plea bargain. Yet, if you look at the table, it's obvious that there is a better option for each of them, if they could only talk to each other, and then act in their *common* interest, rather than each in his *own* best interest. If they agree to hold out, protesting innocence (forget the morality of the situation), they will end up in jail for only two years, not five.

Game theorists use the term *dominant strategy* to describe a competitive situation in which a player finds that his own best decision doesn't depend on what the others do. This has been a case in which each player's dominant strategy has been clear enough, yet each could actually do better if they cooperated with each other. That may appear self-contradictory, but is not—when individual decisions are correlated the options expand.

Even worse, this is a situation that invites duplicity. Suppose that, despite the best efforts of the jailers, Jerry and Keith do manage to communicate, perhaps by tapping on the cell walls. Or perhaps through a small bribe to a jailer. They might then agree that their best bet is to stick to their denials, through thick and thin. Even if they start out on that track, it is still in the best interest of either of them to secretly confess at the last minute, hoping for a thirty-day sentence. Their trust in each other would have to be great indeed to accept this risk. It is the same for two hostile countries that agree to mutual disarmament: the advantage goes to the one that cheats. Countries keep relearning this one the hard way. Some never do learn, but natural selection keeps the number of those down.

A more elaborate social version of the same dilemma, for more than two players, was described by Garrett Hardin in his famous 1968 essay *Tragedy of the Commons,* using the case of a group of herdsmen whose flocks graze a common pasture. It is in each herdsman's best interest to increase the size of his own herd, but if they *all* do so it will spell tragedy for the pasture, and therefore for each of them individually. And if they do agree to limit the size of their herds, the one who cheats will prosper. Consider the unsolved problem of human overpopulation of the earth, where the same principles are in play.

The fact that self-interest can work against the common good is far-reaching, and no general solution is known. Even when everyone agrees that a public work is desirable, it is in the self-interest of each individual to pay as little as possible for it. It is in deference to that inescapable fact that it is legal for us to avoid taxes, but not to evade them. And it is why, in our democratic society, people seem willing to vote for virtually all socially beneficial projects, provided only that they benefit, and that someone else pays.

There is no real escape from the Prisoners' Dilemma, since only collusion can lead to a common decision to stand fast. And even collusion, in the real world, may not, in the long run, be stable—it must survive the stresses of enlightened self-interest. The analogy to real life, and to treaties between nations, is pretty obvious. This was well understood by Aristotle a couple of thousand years ago. He regarded mob rule as the natural end game of a democracy, and gave that condition the marvelous name *ochlocracy*. Of course, he was fluent in Greek.

8

Competitive Games

So far there has been no competition in our decision-making problems—no one working against us. Nature and the laws of probability themselves don't take sides—they don't care whether we win or lose. But the dream that we are in charge of our own destinies while the rest of the world is indifferent is unrealistic; competition for survival has been the stuff of life as far back as we have any knowledge of human, or for that matter plant and animal, history. That's a million years or so for humans, depending on what we mean by human, more for the other life-forms. Presumably the reason our species came to its present (and precarious) dominant position on the planet was not that our ancestors could leap higher or run faster or bite and claw better than the competition, but that they were somehow more adaptable to changing situations and environments. It's a moot question whether they could have survived the catastrophe that wiped out the dinosaurs some 70 million years ago—our kind came too late for that—but their ability to use tools to deal with their environmental and nutritional challenges dates from the earliest Paleolithic period. Development of higher skills was a slow process, but it did proceed, driven by the evolutionary struggle for survival. Despite the babbling of the creationists, evolution is inevitable in a competitive world, and it does work. The fittest, like it or not, have a better chance of surviving and, even more important, reproducing. (There are creatures for whom reproduction is fatal, but they do it anyway.) Take away the advantage of the fittest, and evolution stops. It may even regress as a consequence of the second law of thermodynamics, but that's a different subject.

That honing of human character over the ages has made us (the survivors) competitive animals. Competitive games provide models for real life, and their study helps us understand decision making in an environment in which other participants may be—and probably are—working against us. Strangely, serious efforts to analyze even the simplest competitive games—those against a thinking adversary—date only from the first half of this century. The landmark contribution was the inscrutable book *Theory of Games and Economic Behavior,* by John von Neumann and Oskar Morgenstern in 1944, with a later edition in 1947, and there have been hundreds of books since. Von Neumann, who had written some papers on the subject in the 1920s, was one of the truly brilliant—and we never use that term lightly—mathematicians of the twentieth century, while Morgenstern was a noted economist. The combination of subjects in their title emphasizes the fact that the theory of games has important practical applications—it's been the economists who have taken it up with fervor. This chapter will be devoted almost entirely to the simplest case: two-player zero-sum games. They illustrate the general principles very well, with a minimum of excess baggage. It gets much harder with more players, and many problems remain unsolved.

Here's the simplest of all possible two-player games. You extend your closed hands with, say, a pebble hidden in one of them. If I guess which hand has the pebble, I win something—say, a dime. If I guess wrong, I lose a dime. The odds seem to be even, and it is a zero-sum game. (Anything I win, you lose, and vice versa.) There appears to be no skill involved—I can guess by flipping a coin or by consulting my navel, as long as I don't have x-ray eyes or prior knowledge about which hand holds the pebble. But that's true only the first few times. If I notice (to pick an extreme case) that you prefer your right hand, or that you tend to alternate hands between tries, or have any other recognizable pattern, I'll soon catch on, begin outguessing you, and start winning. And if you notice that I usually pick the left hand, or alternate hands on each pick, or whatever, you'll begin to play to frustrate me. If I manage to avoid showing a pattern you can exploit, it's clearly in your best interest to avoid one yourself, lest I catch on. It is in each of our best interests to notice when the other develops predictable habits.

It is when that contest of guessing sets in that intelligence begins to pay off. Despite the simple rules, this is a challenging game. (About forty years ago, a guessing machine to play the game against humans was built at the Bell Telephone Laboratories by Claude Shannon, a gifted mathematician who was the creator of modern information theory. The machine was amazingly successful in direct competition with real people, who have trouble concealing their patterns.) The best strategy in this game, for each player, is to look for a pattern in the other's behavior, and therefore the best counterstrategy for each is to behave as randomly as possible—to avoid visible patterns—while exploiting the other's weaknesses. (That's true of most competitive games: Football teams try their best to mix up running and passing plays, and talented baseball pitchers mix fast balls and curve balls. And good poker players don't bluff too often. But if they do it only when it is unexpected, that, too, is a pattern.) If the two pebble players can randomize their actions with equal skill, they will break even in the long run. Skill in the game means learning to exploit the other player's predictability, while otherwise behaving unpredictably yourself. Try it; it's a good competitive thinking game. (The Shannon machine had a string of impressive wins before it finally lost a match against a company executive whose thought patterns were extremely random. Is there a lesson there?)

Now let's try something a bit more substantial, for which we need to name some competitors—say, Jack and Jill. Again, it will be a zero-sum game, but with more options. The layout will be like the decision-making pattern of Jerry and Keith in the last chapter, but instead of jail terms for each player, there will be competitive moves by the competing players. No communication is allowed—since they are competitors they don't want to divulge their strategies anyway. The picture will look like this, with Jack's possible moves labeled A through D, and Jill's E through H. The game is simply that Jill secretly picks a row (a horizontal line) and Jack independently picks a column (a vertical line), with the outcome of that round depending on what is in the square at the intersection when the moves are revealed. (Say they submit their moves in sealed envelopes, which are then opened by the judge.)

Jack

		A	B	C	D
	E	56	32	27	60
Jill	F	63	2	19	15
	G	2	29	23	38
	H	26	10	21	49

The number in each square is Jill's gain for that particular pair of choices, and is correspondingly Jack's loss. We've picked the numbers more or less at random. (Not entirely, of course—authors always reserve the right to doctor their numbers to make a point.) Both players know the stakes—they have this very diagram in front of them. We biased the game in Jill's favor by using only positive numbers—the way it reads, she can't lose. That doesn't change the conclusions we'll draw; it just avoids the minor nuisance of negative numbers. Jill will want to maximize her gains, and Jack to minimize them. (To make it more realistic, suppose that she pays Jack a flat fee for admission to the game, and hopes to make it back in winnings.) We've also chosen a square table—each player has the same number of choices—but that isn't necessary. If one were the offensive team in a football game, and the other the defensive team, they would have entirely different lists of options. (Competitive sports like football can be thought of as zero-sum games, because any points scored by one team could just as well be thought of as negative points for the other. The one with the most points at the end wins. There are sports in which you can score negative points, usually through penalties.)

Now Jill's job is to think of her best move, not knowing what Jack will do (and conversely, of course). No collusion—they unveil their moves at the same time. Jill might be inclined to go for a big win by picking F, hoping that Jack will oblige by choosing A, thereby awarding her a score of 63, the best available. But Jack is no idiot, and also knows what is in the table, so he just might guess her move and choose B for himself, dropping her gain to a paltry 2, hardly worth her effort. On thinking over Jack's possible countermoves to her move, Jill may well decide to play conservatively, and to choose her move to maximize her gains regardless of what Jack does. That way she'll be giving him credit for some intelligence, and trying to allow for it. She can do this by looking at each row (a horizontal line) that represents a possible move for her, and picking the one whose *minimum,* representing Jack's best move against hers, is as large as possible. That would be called a maximin strategy—she would be trying to maximize the minimum gain that Jack could hold her to. With this kind of thinking, she would be inclined to choose option E, because the smallest number in that row, 27, representing the worst she can do if her move is E, is larger than the smallest number in any other row. Nothing Jack can do on his move can reduce her gain below 27, whereas any other move on her part would leave her vulnerable to Jack's unpredictable counterplay.

Notice that this logic is not the same as the logic we used in speaking of probabilities earlier, where the objective was to get the largest *expected* gain, given the odds on each possible outcome of a decision. Nature and the laws of probability are trustworthy and play no favorites, but a malicious opponent changes everything. What Jill has done is to look for the worst treatment that Jack can inflict on her, and make that as good as possible. It is a conservative approach, sometimes called worst-case planning, and is not uncommon in real life. It reflects an aversion to losing, rather than a zeal for winning. For such an objective, a maximin strategy makes sense for Jill.

We still haven't looked at this game from Jack's point of view. He, of course, wants to minimize his losses to Jill, so he might be inclined to adopt a minimax strategy, looking for the *maximum* in each *column* (vertical line) that he can pick, and picking the column that *minimizes* that number. That would be the exact complement to Jill's strategy, and would amount to making his own worst case as good as possible. He's giving Jill credit for doing as well as she can, just trying to make that as unrewarding for her as possible. Well, the smallest maximum that Jack can find in a column is the 27 in column C, so if he were to choose C, nothing Jill could do—no row she could pick—could cost him more than 27 points. In his own best interests, again acting conservatively, Jack is likely to choose C, while Jill, acting conservatively in her own best interests, is likely to choose E.

The upshot will be that Jill will win 27 of whatever is at stake, the minimum she had counted on, while Jack has held his loss to the maximum planned level, also 27. We might call this a stable game, since each player's optimal move turns out to have been the best, even when the other's move is finally revealed. In fact, the moves don't even have to be hidden in this case—nothing Jack can do will improve the outcome for him, even after he knows Jill's move. And conversely, knowing Jack's move wouldn't change Jill's decision at all.

But it is a coincidence that, in this case, the maximin strategy practiced by Jill leads to exactly the same result as the minimax strategy practiced by Jack—a net score of 27—and that neither Jack nor Jill can assure a better outcome. The key word is *assure*, since there are many combinations of moves that would produce larger or smaller numbers if one player played badly. After all, the smallest and largest numbers in the table are 2 and 63, and each represents a possible combination of moves. Yet at a score of 27 each player has done as well as possible, while giving the opposition some credit for intelligence. Since it is normally (but not always) unwise to count on your opponent's incompetence, it is prudent for Jill to play E and for Jack to play C. The game is stable.

But that was a coincidence, sneakily arranged by the author. Suppose the 19 and the 27 in the C column had been interchanged, as in the second table.

Jack

		A	B	C	D
	E	56	32	19	60
	F	63	2	27	15
Jill	G	2	29	23	38
	H	26	10	21	49

Then the same reasoning as before would lead Jack to play C with a minimax strategy, and still with a maximum expected loss of 27, while Jill would still be led to a maximin at E, but now with a minimum expected gain of 19. If each played according to the previous pattern, Jill would now win only 19 instead of the previous 27. But in this case there is nothing automatic about the reasoning—it is a real game. Jill might imagine herself in Jack's place, understand the reasoning that might drive him to C, and therefore cleverly pick F for herself. She would be risking a gain of only 2 if Jack saw through this strategy and selected B, but would win the full 27 if he didn't. Of course, she might assume that Jack thinks he can predict that line of thought, and might therefore select B. If he really tried that, she might then be able to outwit him at the next level by playing her original choice of E. He would then be outwitting himself. And so forth. In any competitive game in which all the facts are laid out on the table (chess, for instance), this kind of plotting and counterplotting is the whole point of the game, and those who do it best, and plan the most moves ahead, win. This is a one-move game, so there is not much memory involved, but chess and go are games of many moves, in which the number of possibilities quickly gets out of hand if you try to think too far ahead. Even the good chess-playing computer programs make no pretense of evaluating all possible moves. But they are beating chess grandmasters pretty regularly these days. Not always, but regularly.

But that's not the end of it. There is an even better way to play in an unstable game, and that was von Neumann's great contribution.

We learned from the pebble-in-the-hand game that it is sometimes useful to adopt a random strategy, just to frustrate an opponent who can improve his position by guessing your move. The Jack-and-Jill game is no exception, though the mathematics needed to make the case precisely goes beyond our ambitions for this book. Still, we can see intuitively how it works if we change the rules of the game just a bit. Instead of requiring that Jack and Jill choose a single option each, we'll let them hedge their bets. For Jack, for example, instead of having to choose A, B, C, or D, he may be able to put half his bet on A, none on B, and a quarter on each of C and D—or any combination he likes—and similarly for Jill. Think of each of them having a pile of chips to bet with, as in roulette.

Now go back to Jill's strategy for the unstable version of the game, the second table above. Her problem was that her best maximin strategy would lead her to move E, which, combined with Jack's best minimax move of C, would allow her to win only 19 points. If she had *really* been sure that Jack would choose C, she'd have been better off with F, winning 27 points. Why not, then, cover both possibilities by putting a fraction of her chips on each? For example, she might put two-thirds of her chips on E and one-third on F, as a hedge against Jack's sneakiness. Then, if Jack goes ahead with the expected choice of C, she'll hit 19 with two-thirds of her stake, and 27 with the other third, for a total of about 21.7. That's a good deal better than the originally guaranteed 19. And if Jack actually tries to fool her by playing B, she will land on 32 with the first two-thirds, and only 2 with the rest, but still with a total of 22, better still. (For the purists, this isn't quite the optimal betting strategy for Jill, but it's close, and the choice of a truly perfect strategy really does require slightly fancier mathematics.)

Of course, Jack hasn't been daydreaming through all this; he knows Jill has that kind of hedge available, and can distribute his own bets to limit her winnings. He might put some chips on C, as the best conservative move, but some fraction on B to counter Jill's most likely strategy. We leave it to the reader to work out how he can improve his position over simply putting his whole bet on one column. The upshot is that, for *any* game of this kind, whether or not it is stable for single bets, there is an optimal way for each player to hedge, leading to a stable situation.

That is the central theorem about two-player zero-sum games. There is an optimal hedged strategy for each player, and each can optimize his position regardless of the other's betting. Only rarely is it best to put all your eggs in one basket. It's not obvious, but there you are. It remains only to say that the relaxation of the rules that gave the players the ability to split their bets really wasn't necessary if the game is to be played often enough. Jill could have bet on E two-thirds of the time, and F one-third of the time, being careful to mix up her bets randomly, and that would have been just as good as splitting the bet, in the long run. On any single play, of course, it would be a gamble. And the best counterstrategy for Jack would be to mix up his bets, lest Jill learn his pattern. Experts on game theory would call such randomized choices mixed strategies.

The analysis of zero-sum games with more than two players is more complex, and we will pass up the chance to alienate too many readers so early in the book. Most of the principles will show up in time, in our treatment of multiparty strategies. It is, however, worth noting one special feature of three-party games, which will surface again in our discussion of Lanchester's law in Chapter 16. It is *always* a good strategy for two players to join forces (or conspire) against the third, and to settle their own differences when he has been done in. With suitable variations, that lesson applies to games with more and more players, to say nothing, alas, of life.

9

A Paradox

Here is an interesting so-called paradox, easy to describe, that still produces fits among professional statisticians and decision theorists.

A paradox is an *apparent* self-contradiction. Real self-contradiction is impossible, and the main role of paradoxes in studies of logic (and rational decision making depends on logic, as does all rational thinking) is to challenge our coherence—to make sure we have the pegs in their right holes. It seems pretty obvious that two statements that contradict each other can't both be right—a coin can't land both heads and tails on the same toss—so a standard test for the self-consistency of a logical system is to show that whatever else you think you can do, you can't prove two statements that are clearly opposites. The road to madness is to disagree with yourself and let it go at that, but one step on the road to wisdom is to resolve *apparent* internal disagreements. The great genius Albert Einstein spent a substantial part of his middle years trying to invent paradoxes that would show that quantum mechanics (a new theory he had helped develop, but with which he later felt uncomfortable) wasn't self-consistent. He failed, and quantum mechanics is still around, though it still challenges those who think deeply about Einstein's paradoxes and their sequelae. He was a true genius, and the resolution of his paradoxes took the best that the world of physics had to offer in those days. Some of his paradoxes still remain troublesome to experts—those who claim they are not troubled cannot be experts.

A good example of a logical paradox, and probably the granddaddy of them all, is the Epimenides paradox. Epimenides was a Cretan with a somewhat obscure history, who lived about twenty-five hundred years ago. He is purported to have said, "All Cretans are liars," and that, in a nutshell, is the classic form of the paradox. Is the statement true or false? If it is true, then you cannot believe the speaker, who is Cretan. So it cannot be true. But then it must be a lie, so the speaker is a liar, and how can we believe anything he says about Cretans, including the assertion that they are all liars? It is easy to extend and improve this germ of an idea. This book could contain a sentence telling you to believe nothing in the book, including that sentence. It was an expansion of the central ideas that grow out of the Epimenides paradox that led the iconoclastic mathematician Kurt Gödel to his famous and revolutionary 1931 theorem that all mathematical systems contain theorems that can be neither proved nor disproved. (His theorem isn't one of those—he proved it.) That shocked mathematicians, who had long believed that real mathematics had no such problems—that all theorems could be proved to be either true or false. The existence of undecidables was a surprise—Gödel gave an explicit example—and it revealed some very deep truths about mathematics.

Back to Epimenides. At this point you may be thinking, aha, this sneaky author thought he could put something over on me. Despite twenty-five hundred years of history, there really is no Epimenides paradox, because all Epimenides said was that all Cretans are liars, and this proves that, though he himself is a liar, there is somewhere a truthful Cretan. Then what he said was a lie, but so what? And indeed, that is a way out of the classic version. But change it just a bit, to have him say, "This statement is a lie," or "This Cretan is a liar," and we're back in the soup. That makes the statement entirely self-contained, and is the real core of the paradox. Or you could go to the next step and have two sentences, in which the first says that the second is false, and the second says that the first is true. And on and on. So the classic version is just a matter of sloppy workmanship; the paradox is intact. And indeed self-reference in mathematics was the basis of Gödel's proof.

But that's a digression. Paradoxes play an important role in protecting us from loose thinking, and here's a decision-theoretic paradox, cast in terms similar to those of the last chapter. Don't expect the resolution to be obvious.

The two players, Bill and Coo, are sipping sherry in the garden while discussing ancient myths about genies. Soon a real genie is attracted by the conversation, materializes behind a bush, listens for a while, and is impressed by the depth of their knowledge. He wants to reward them for their scholarship, but rather than grant them the traditional three wishes, he decides to be more pragmatic, so he writes two checks (he has an account at a Swiss bank). He shuffles the checks, puts each into a sealed envelope, and gives the checks to the two players in random order. As he vanishes in the traditional puff of smoke, he is heard to say that the two checks are for different sums, and that one is exactly twice as large as the other. But he says nothing more about their value.

After his departure each player secretly looks at his own check, and begins to wonder if he got the short or the long end of the deal.

Bill thinks to himself: My check is for a magnificent sum, especially for a windfall, but Coo's check must be for either half as much (if I got the biggie) or twice as much (if he got the benefit of the draw). Besides, the way it was done—the two checks were written and shuffled before they were given to us—it must be even money which of us got the bigger check. But that means I should offer to trade with Coo, since I would have an even chance of either doubling my money or losing half of it, and that means a net expected gain. (If you have ten dollars, and are given a chance to flip a coin to determine whether you will win ten more dollars or lose five dollars of your ten, accept the offer, and rejoice in your understanding of probability. And forget for the moment what we said in Chapter 4 about the utility of money.) So Bill decides, using decision-theoretic principles, that it's to his advantage to trade with Coo. In fact, it seems that he could have made this decision without ever opening his envelope—the amount in it didn't matter to the logic.

But Coo has gone through exactly the same thinking, and has concluded that it's to *his* advantage to trade with Bill. So he jumps at the chance when Bill suggests a trade. Each is in the same position as the other, each thinks he has correctly estimated the probabilities and the utilities, each is convinced that he should trade, and each has apparently obeyed the rules of logic. Can they both be right? After all, this is a zero-sum game; Bill's gain is Coo's loss, and vice versa, so they can't both win. Someone must be wrong, yet each has gone through the same apparently unimpeachable logical chain. There is of course nothing *logically* wrong with a contest in which both sides are convinced they'll win—that happens more often than not in sports, love affairs, and wars. But in this case each of the players is supposed to be functioning rationally. That's the paradox.

Now the resolution. Think before you read further. Have a cup of tea. Hug a child or special friend. Many incorrect articles in learned journals have been published on this one, so it is worth a bit of thought.

Both Bill and Coo have committed the cardinal sin of believing that the probability of having the big prize is the same after the envelopes are distributed and opened as it was before. The genie carefully shuffled the envelopes before handing them over, so it is completely true that, *before* the distribution, each player had a fifty-fifty chance of getting the big one. But that doesn't mean that either Bill or Coo can look at his envelope and conclude that there is still an even chance that the envelope he's holding in his hand has the smaller share in it.

Think of it this way. Whatever the genie decides to give away, whether it be $1,000 or $1,000,000,000 (a billion), once he has divided the loot into two unequal packages and shuffled them, Bill is as likely to get one as the other. No problem there. But once the envelopes have been distributed and inspected it's a different story.

Remember that neither Bill nor Coo has the foggiest notion of the size of the genie's bank account (Swiss banks keep their little secrets), or even of his level of generosity—he keeps his magnanimity to himself. All they can possibly know is what they see in their own little envelopes. So if Bill looks into his envelope, and finds a check for $100,000, all he really knows is that there are two possibilities for the genie's largesse: if Coo got $50,000 then the genie gave away $150,000, *but* if Coo has $200,000 then the genie gave away $300,000, and he (Bill) got the smaller amount. So the odds he has to estimate are not whether he got the smaller or larger of a fixed amount (which was truly even money before the distribution), but whether the genie gave away

$150,000 or $300,000. That's a completely different set of alternatives, and Bill has no reason at all to believe they have equal probabilities. In fact, if he assumes that even genies have a limit to their wealth (or generosity), he would be better off to assume the worst: that the genie is more likely to have gone for the smaller sum, so he probably already has the bigger bundle, and ought to stay put. That's the opposite of what he thought in the first place.

He might, of course, think that genies are so very rich that neither $150,000 nor $300,000 means much to them, so the probabilities are really about equal, as he thought in the first place, and again it makes sense to trade. The hooker is that he can't go on and on saying that, into the millions or billions of dollars, simply because we are talking probabilities here, and the sum of all probabilities *must* add up to one. That's a basic law of probability, and neither Bill, nor Coo, nor the genie, can violate it. If all probabilities are the same, no matter how much money we're talking about, then they can't add up to one. That means that both Bill and Coo *must*, if they want to make rational decisions, make some kind of estimate of the limits on the genie's wealth and propensity for largesse, and whoever does it best, matching that estimate against the size of his own gift, will make the best decision about trading. The one with the smaller sum in his envelope will probably be more willing to trade, and that is entirely reasonable.

But will either of them be right about the actual probability? Probably not, given their limited experience with genies' bank accounts and charitable impulses. But so what? Just as in real life, the one who can make the best estimate will make the best decision. The original argument that the odds were even in the distribution of envelopes was simply misleading: it compared the wrong set of alternatives. It was a red herring.

There is an important lesson here, that when you speak of probability you have to be clear about the alternatives whose probabilities you are comparing. The probabilities that were indeed even money were the probabilities that Bill or Coo would be given the big envelope. But once done, that set of alternatives no longer exists, and there is no meaning to probabilities for things that have already been decided. So probabilities change on the fly as events unfold, options change or are eliminated, and so forth. Once the envelopes have been distributed, the options for which probabilities exist are options about how much money the genie has distributed, not who got what.

So there is no real paradox, and the lesson is that it is easy to be fooled into mistaking a priori (before the fact) probabilities for one set of options for a posteriori (after the fact) probabilities about another set. They can be very different. No racetrack will let you bet on the race as the horses come thundering down the stretch. That seems so obvious that it is embarrassing to say it, yet it's the root of the paradox of this chapter. Stay on your toes for this one—it is probably the most common mistake in popular misuse of probabilities. A probability is the relative chance for one event, in a sea of other possible events. You need to know both to use a probability properly.

10

Rankings

Up to now we've dealt mostly with cases in which there is some way to put a specific value on the consequences of a decision. That's wonderful when it can be done, but it's not always practical or even possible. In some cases it isn't even necessary. If you have limited resources, and are trying to decide whether to use them to buy a yacht or to send the children to college, you shouldn't have to go through an elaborate analysis to know where to make your commitment. There are times when simple preferences are perfectly adequate for decision making—a choice of date, a book to read, or a snack from the refrigerator. Then the choice between any pair of options simply comes down to which you prefer—a ranking. We handle elections this way when we ask the voters to express nothing more than their preference among the candidates for office. There may be multiple contenders, or complex schemes of proportional representation, where the simple choice doesn't provide all the information that might be useful, but in the United States we rarely use them. (More about that in the next chapter.) We ask voters whether they prefer Smith to Jones, not *how much* they prefer Smith to Jones. A lukewarm vote gets just as much weight as an enthusiastic vote. (Pollsters do sometimes ask the pollee whether the view expressed is strongly held. That gets extra points in a poll, but not in an election.) To top it all off, when we do finally total up the votes in a preference election, we discount the size of a winning candidate's majority, as long as we have a winner. So a passionate minority can beat a docile majority in a revolution, an insurrection, or a riot, but not in an election. (The winner of an election will, of course, always claim a "popular mandate," no

matter how tiny and fragile his winning margin, or how scur-
rilously assembled.)

If a preference is a matter of individual taste or judgment, it
is hardly open to dispute. When George Will says he prefers the
Chicago Cubs to the Los Angeles (née Brooklyn) Dodgers, one
can marvel at his perversity, but it is futile to argue. *Sobre gustas
no hay disputa*. Determining the preferences of an individual
may be just a matter of asking the right question, but determining
the preferences of a *group* of people is not a simple matter. And
that's what social choice (including elections) is all about.

We've mentioned the problem of the choice of ice-cream flavor if our preferences, or rankings, are intransitive. There is
nothing irrational about being intransitive—we may simply be
using different criteria in each pair comparison—but it does
complicate decision making. Even when individual decision
makers (voters or committee members, for example) are individually transitive—have straightforward preference lists—new
problems appear when we try to mold the individual lists into a
group preference list.

The two problems we'll deal with here are the rankings
problem and the Condorcet problem. The first deals with the issue of how to turn individual rankings into group rankings, and
the second with the remarkable fact that when you assemble a
group of individually transitive preferences into a group ranking,
the result need not be transitive. Actually, the point is even
stronger than that, as we'll soon see. Just to be clear, when we say
individual or group rankings we are not describing the items being ranked; it is those doing the ranking who may be either individuals or groups.

Suppose we are on the faculty of a university, and have the
perennial problem of choosing among the students for some
honor—say, the award of a scholarship. There are several students with records good enough to make them credible candidates, and the faculty members have the responsibility of choosing among them. It is not easy to rank students. Quality involves
more than just grades received in courses (some students take
only easy courses) or classroom personality (some students are
awfully good at buttering up professors). A professor's job is to
assess real quality and potential from a variety of clues, all of
which contribute to a ranking, and few of which may be trace-

able. So there is often little choice but to ask each individual faculty member to rank the students in order by some subjective standard, and then try to use the individual rankings in some reasonable way to choose the honoree. Each faculty member's list will, of course, be transitive—no list should circle back on itself. Will that reasonable way to combine reasonable lists always lead to a conclusion that reasonably summarizes the individually reasonable views of the group? By no means.

A marvelous set of papers was written on the subject by an English cleric and mathematician of the nineteenth century, the Reverend Charles Lutwidge Dodgson (better known to most of us under his pen name of Lewis Carroll, creator of Alice in Wonderland). He was originally motivated by the problem of choosing a belfry for his college, a job that had been assigned to a committee, but extended his interest to the problem of choosing students for particular honors, the case we'll use here. All he sought was to find a fair and unambiguous way to do the job. He knew about the problems of transitivity, but thought he could use his mathematical skills to devise an acceptable voting method. To his surprise and annoyance, it wasn't possible, and we could do worse than make the case with Dodgson's own first example. Here it is, and we'll do it his way.

There are eleven electors (faculty) and four candidates (students), and each elector ranks the candidates in order of preference. We'll start by counting only first-place votes, the way we run most American elections, but will come back to the full rankings later. No individual elector here has a transitivity problem—if he prefers a to b and also b to c, then he prefers a to c. No games—there is a real order of preference. The winner will be the candidate with the most first-place votes, and that will be that. Suppose the individual rankings come out as follows, where each column is the rating list for one elector, and the candidates are named a, b, c, and d.

a	a	a	b	b	b	b	c	c	c	d
c	c	c	a	a	a	a	a	a	a	a
d	d	d	c	c	c	c	d	d	d	c
b	b	b	d	d	d	d	b	b	b	b

According to the rule of only counting first-place votes, candidate b is elected with four votes. No one else has more than three first-place votes, but this is clearly a terrible mistake. Every single elector who didn't think him best rated him worst of all—he has fans, but most people have a very low opinion of him—and that ought to have had some weight. It isn't counted if only first-place votes matter. So let's go a step further, and compare b to each of the other candidates in turn, asking how many of the electors prefer him. In these head-to-head comparisons b loses to *each* of the other candidates by the same seven-to-four score. (That's obvious, since he was rated last by seven electors.) He won a plurality of first-place votes, yet each of the other candidates is preferred to him by a solid majority of the electors. Any way you slice it, most people think he's a bum. It doesn't make much sense to elect him, and Dodgson said so. You lose a lot of information by counting only first-place votes.

But which candidate really does seem best, by more expansive criteria? Candidate a was chosen first by three of the electors and second by every single one of the others. No one rated him below second place, so he would seem to be a reasonable consensus choice. He also *won* head-to-head contests with each and every one of the others, though not as decisively as b lost. In a direct comparison of a and b, seven of the eleven preferred a. In a runoff between the top two vote-getters (the rule in many foreign countries and in some American states and municipalities), a would have won in a landslide.

Even if we insist that the winner have an absolute majority, or use a runoff, neglect of second and third choices can lead to inequity. Using the same table, we can imagine a runoff between the top two first-place vote-getters, a and b, and imagine that in that runoff the four first-place votes that went to c and d were divided equally between a and b. Then b would have a bare absolute majority, so he would win the runoff. If, on the other hand, all the disappointed voters for c and d were to vote their earlier preferences between a and b, then a would get all those votes (b was last on all those ballots), and a would win. So a runoff does indeed provide some information beyond straight first-place voting.

It's even worse than it looks. Remember that you want to count all the electors equally, so you would surely want to have the same outcome if several of the electors mixed up their voting sheets, but the whole package ended up with the same number preferring a to b, and so forth, as before. In other words, if you don't care about the identity of the electors, the preferences in the voting can be summarized by six numbers, how many votes there are for a over b, c over d, and so forth, and you shouldn't care how these preferences are distributed among the electors' ballots. There is, as mathematicians would have it, a many-to-one mapping problem here. (If you consider how many possible ways votes could be cast in such an election, you could find out the same way we did poker hands back in Chapter 3. With eleven electors, all nameless, you'd end up with 38,121,292 different ways this election could come out. But if all you really care about is how many voters prefer, say, a to b, and so on, that's only six numbers, rating the six possible pairings of four candidates.) So there are many possible tables like the one above, leading to exactly the same preference list, yet yielding different outcomes of the election for different rules. Dodgson gave one example.

a	a	a	a	a	a	a	b	b	b	b
c	c	c	c	c	c	c	d	c	c	c
d	d	d	d	d	d	d	a	a	a	a
b	b	b	b	b	b	b	c	d	d	d

The new table leads to *exactly* the same preference list as the previous one (e.g., ten of the eleven voters prefer a to d in each list), yet by any set of reasonable rules candidate a would surely win this election. He would have lost before, yet it's the same information if all you care about is rankings.

Dodgson considered the usual variety of options: eliminating the worst performers one at a time, runoffs, and so forth. He finally concluded that there is really no satisfactory way to choose a winner when several decision makers have to choose among several options. He ended with a preference for a particular method we won't even mention, but his real contribution was that nothing really works. And this was without transitivity problems.

We promised that we would also show that a group could be intransitive, even when its members were not. That will play a larger role later, in the context of voting systems and of Arrow's impossibility theorem, but let's get a taste here.

Consider the simplest case of three voters, with three options, leading to a preference table like the ones we've been using. Nothing could be simpler.

a	b	c
b	c	a
c	a	b

Just by making the table in which we write the choices in a column we've guaranteed that no individual voter has a problem with transitivity; for example, the first voter prefers a to b to c, and therefore prefers a to c. Each voter is entirely self-consistent, but his specific preferences are his own business. Now suppose we innocently believe in popular democracy, so the majority rules absolutely, and all we count are preferences. We see that two out of three voters prefer a to b, while two out of three prefer b to c, and two out of three prefer c to a, making it a full circle, with no decision possible. So intransitivity is a pernicious problem, emerging in group decisions even when the individuals making up the group have no problem at all.

The upshot is that a voting democracy is easier to talk about than it is to implement, and the built-in ambiguities of ranking systems provide ample opportunity for astute participants to manipulate the results of an otherwise fair selection process, within any set of rules. Despite all the talk about the "will of the people" in stump speeches, it is not easy—in fact, it's impossible—to determine what that will is. It is easier to declare yourself a democracy (though, as we mentioned earlier, the United States has never done so) than it is to implement that declaration. We obviously have to go into this kind of decision problem more deeply, and soon will.

11

Voting

Do all the problems we talked about in the last chapter really apply to the honest-to-golly political world? The 1992 presidential election (the most recent available when this was written) gave the three major candidates the following percentages of the popular and electoral votes:

Candidate	Popular	Electoral
Bill Clinton	43	69
George Bush	38	31
Ross Perot	19	0

so, according to our Constitution, Bill Clinton was elected president of the United States, with more than two-thirds of the electoral votes. By comparison, he had much less than half the popular vote, quite a difference. Ross Perot, favored by nearly a fifth of the voting population, got no electoral votes at all. The rules, dating from the original Constitution in 1789, and amended fifteen years later, award the job to the candidate with a majority (more than half) of the electoral votes, if there is such a candidate. If no candidate has a majority of the electoral votes, the Constitution has a complex procedure that takes the choice completely out of the hands of the voters, both popular and electoral. (Thomas Jefferson won his first term as president through this procedure.) Though it was not anticipated by the authors of the Constitution, the individuality of the electors has itself been eroded by time, and their names are not even on the election ballots in most states. In nearly all cases they run as a group, pledged to support the candidate of their party, and only rarely has an elector broken that pledge. The direct consequence is that every single one of the electoral votes of a particular state goes to the winning candidate in that state, and a bare plurality of the popular vote in a populous state can overwhelm large majorities in smaller states. The losing voters in a state have no further influence on the choice of president—they lost their chance when their own slate of electors was defeated. (At this writing, only Maine and Nebraska deviate from the winner-take-all pattern.) It is therefore possible (and it happened in 1992) for a candidate with a clear minority of the popular votes across the nation to have a majority of the electoral votes (in this case a vast majority). It has happened sixteen times in our history, usually (but not always) when a third political party siphoned off popular votes from the major candidates. In the 1992 election, President Clinton received a majority of the popular vote in only three states and the District of Columbia. The states were Maryland, New York, and his home state of Arkansas.

Though the writers of the Constitution intended that the electors have minds of their own, and not be mindless herds in bondage to the political parties, that hasn't been the case for many a moon (with a few exceptions). The Constitution doesn't even specify how the electors are to be chosen—each state is left to its own devices, subject only to the requirement that the state legislature prescribe the system. It would apparently not be unconstitutional for the state legislature to delegate the job to the faculty of the state university, or to the mascot of the football team, or even to the football team itself. (Relax, we could depend on the Supreme Court to declare it unconstitutional, regardless of the facts.)

It is different for the Senate and the House of Representatives. The original Constitution specified that each state's representatives should be chosen by the people of the state (the word *election* is not used, but the writers had some kind of popular choice in mind). The senators, on the other hand, were to be chosen by the legislature, whose members were in turn to be chosen however the state wished to choose them, within some bounds. It was a clear effort on the part of the Founding Fathers to dilute direct public participation in the selection of the members of Congress. The Constitution was later amended to provide for popular choice of the senators, too, specifically by election. Even with the word *election*, it is clear from the last chapter that there is a lot of potential for manipulation in the definition of a group choice.

Political scientists have long wrestled with the problem of the "best" way to make this kind of decision, where the complex wishes of the public are hard to determine in a straight up/down vote, and the need for a functional government may also take some priority over immediate public desires. (We all know of countries with dysfunctional governments. Opinions are divided on whether we're there yet.) The original Constitution specified that in the presidential election each elector would vote for two names, with the majority vote-getter selected as president and the runner-up vice-president. That may at first blush seem fairer than simply disenfranchising the minority, but it was soon seen to lead to contentious and ineffective government, and the Constitution was quickly amended to lead to our present system, starting with the election of 1804. (Imagine having Ronald Reagan as president and Jimmy Carter as vice-president. Or Bill Clinton as president and George Bush as vice-president. Or Franklin Roosevelt as president, and Herbert Hoover as vice-president. The mind does boggle.) It was one of the very few genuine blunders in the writing of the Constitution. That document represented an impressive achievement, by impressive people.

We've made a big fuss throughout this book about the importance of knowing your objectives *before* making decisions. What is our purpose in selecting a president? Perhaps it would be unwise, for the good of all of us, to determine the will of the people too precisely. The story of the *Tragedy of the Commons* made it clear that a government that is no more than a translation of the individual desires of the population can lead to bad decisions for everyone, even though each individual vote is cast in what is sometimes called enlightened self-interest. Such decisions can be bad even for the self-interested, whether or not enlightened. (We'll come back to this in Chapter 14.) Besides, there are too many of us to make communal decisions. We may even want leaders—perish the thought—who are more competent

than the average among us. So all modern democracies incorpo-
rate some form of representative government, which insulates
the decision makers somewhat from the selectors of the decision
makers—the people. Our Constitution aimed at some such level
of insulation, but it is eroding in this era of instant mass communication, with ominous implications. Representatives now depend heavily on polling to determine their constituents' wishes,
lest they displease a single potential voter. And decision making
in the selection of governments determines the quality of decision making in those governments. These are deep questions, reserved for later.

One personal anecdote, to illustrate the dilemma: This
author underwent what might profanely be called an epiphany a
few years ago, while sitting quietly in an otherwise unremark-
able meeting in Vienna. The meeting was in a large and spectacular hall in a building that had served long ago as one of Empress
Maria Theresa's palaces. The building and the grounds around it
were both grand and beautiful. The epiphany was the sudden re-
alization that such a magnificent structure could not be built in
modern times, anywhere. There is no decision process in a popular democracy that can accommodate any large project, however
worthy, let alone support it over the time necessary for comple-
tion. While this particular building had largely aesthetic value,
the same statement applies to more pragmatic public works like
roads, dams, and bridges. Besides, a society worth preserving
ought to be sufficiently civilized to spend some small fraction of
its resources on cultural and aesthetic matters.

In our modern societies, in the United States and elsewhere,
there are simply too many ways to stop things, and too few to
keep them going. As recently as forty years ago, in this author's
direct memory, that wasn't true. (If the Interstate Highway System were to be proposed now, it wouldn't stand a chance.) There
are few projects favored by enough people strongly enough to
overcome the inevitable opposition. The pharaohs, with complete authority, could build pyramids over decades or longer.
The Roman Catholic Church, with widely accepted authority,
could build cathedrals that took generations to complete, if indeed any cathedral is ever complete. Maria Theresa was empress, and that says it all for her palace. Decision making by large
groups can never lead to venturesome decisions. In the era of

mass communication and polling, politicians who want to keep their jobs (nearly all of them) cannot risk unpopular decisions, and in the end, our government is composed of politicians.

So the ultimate conflict in selecting our executives and lawmakers is about objectives: do we seek the best possible functioning government, which requires some leadership, some vision, and probably some unpopular decisions, or do we want a system that mirrors our own hopes and desires, disenfranchises no one, and properly reflects the spectrum of views among the voters? There are voting schemes that will favor any of these ends.

The most common complaint about winner-take-all elections is that they truly leave large numbers of voters without any further impact. The minority, like a losing army, simply plans for the next contest, and has entirely lost its influence. Even its traditional role of obstruction is assumed with an eye on the next election. While in our country there is probably going to be a next election, in many other countries, both now and in the past and surely in the future, the loss of a single election can mean loss of influence for a very long time. Winning groups like to hold on to power long after their mandates have expired. Though it hasn't happened yet in our country, it is unwise to be complacent about risk. (Even the statement that it hasn't happened yet is open to discussion—the vast majority of incumbent congressmen do manage to get reelected, somehow.)

The extreme alternative to the winner-take-all scheme is that no one's views ought to be ignored in the daily functioning of government, so each party ought to have representation in the governing body (the legislature in a democracy) exactly proportional to its voting strength. If the Perot group had been organized as a political party in 1992, and the relative party strengths were measured by the votes for their presidential candidates (two big ifs), proportional representation would have led to a legislature of about 43 percent Democrats, 38 percent Republicans, and 19 percent Perotistas (with apologies to Argentina). The standard game-theoretic tactic under such circumstances would have been for any two minority groups to cooperate in frustrating the third, producing chaos as the alignment changed over time. Many European countries use such a system, and it has been tried in parts of our country, but the ultimate lesson everywhere has been that effective government requires decisions—choices among options—and choices that have real consequences are not easily made by highly diverse groups. Those who proclaim so loudly and self-righteously that diversity strengthens a society will have trouble finding historical support for the view. Proportional representation makes it harder to trample a minority, but correspondingly harder to effectuate the desires of the majority. Take your choice. It comes down, as usual, to the ends you seek.

Even within groups smaller than a whole country, and even when intransitivity is not relevant, the outcome of an election can depend entirely on the voting rules. Consider an election for some office, in which there are three candidates, Alf, Bob, and Cad. We'll give this one nine voters, whose preferences are shown, as usual, in the table. The numbers in parentheses above the table are the number of voters who marked their ballots as shown. Thus, two voters named Alf as their first choice, Bob as their second, and Cad as their third.

(2)	(3)	(4)
Alf	Bob	Cad
Bob	Alf	Alf
Cad	Cad	Bob

Under a plurality-wins rule, in which only first-place votes count, Cad is the victor, with four votes, while Bob and Alf have three and two, respectively. Clearly, most people don't like Cad, but he has a devoted constituency. That's not at all unusual in the real world. He would be a minority winner, by about the same margin that Bill Clinton had in 1992.

Let's see how some of the other familiar voting systems handle this one. One of the most popular is weighted voting, in which second and third choices are counted, but with lower weight. One might award two points for a first-place vote, one point for second place, and zero for third place. (This is known as Borda's scheme.) Under that scheme it is easy to see that Alf is the clear winner, with eleven points, while Bob and Cad are tied with eight each. The additional support for Alf comes from his second-place finish with seven of the voters, just as it was in the last chapter for the Dodgson examples. He would be more of a consensus candidate than Cad, though fewer voters made him their first choice.

Another voting scheme that is frequently encountered is called preferential voting. In this scheme, the voter marks his ballot with first, second, and lower choices, as in the table. Then, if any candidate has an absolute majority of the first-place votes, he wins. (Our Electoral College follows that part of the rule.) If not, then the candidate with the fewest first-place votes is eliminated from consideration, and his second-place votes are distributed among the remaining candidates, as they are named on the ballots. In this case, the losing candidate in terms of first-place votes is Alf, the previous consensus winner, so his second-place votes are distributed to the appropriate candidate, in this case Bob. That is enough to put Bob over the top, and make him the winner despite his second ranking in original first-place votes. The virtue of such a scheme is that it takes account of the fact that the supporters of Alf would prefer Bob to Cad if their own favorite didn't win. Isn't it fair that that should be taken into account?

So we've now handled exactly the same expression of the wishes of the voters in three different ways, and gotten three different winners, representing three different goals for the election scheme.

But there are still other ways to count the votes. One method that is well regarded by some authorities is called approval voting. In this one, each voter may vote for as many candidates as he wishes, but may cast no more than one vote for any individual candidate. (When people are first told about this, they tend to react by saying that that's unfair, you're letting any voter vote as often as he likes. But that's a misunderstanding. If you cast a vote for each and every candidate, you will have canceled yourself out, and it will be the same as not having voted at all. A vote for any candidate is equivalent to a vote against the others, and there is no advantage at all to casting many votes.) In this method the voter doesn't rank the candidates, but only signals the list of candidates of whom he approves. That is why it is called approval voting, and the winner will be the candidate with the most approvals from the voting population.

How would that have worked here? Well, we haven't given enough information to tell, but suppose that each voter gave his approval votes to the top two candidates on his list, signaling that either of them would be acceptable, but not the bottom choice. Then Alf would be the winner, with nine approval votes (no one listed him at the bottom), compared to five and four for the other two candidates. So approval voting leads, in this case, to the same result as weighted voting, but you shouldn't make too much of this. With three candidates, and four different voting schemes, at least two have to produce the same result.

So with a plurality we elected Cad, with weighted voting we elected Alf, with preferential voting we elected Bob after Alf was eliminated, and approval voting brought us back to Alf. (In this last case, we had to guess how the voters might have signaled their approval.) Who, pray tell, is the "people's choice"?

Believe it or not, it's even worse than that. A very common scheme for multiple candidates, used in many states and municipalities in the United States, and often in parliamentary elections abroad, is the runoff, mentioned in the last chapter. Under that scheme only first-place votes are counted—there is just one vote cast by each voter—and if there is no majority candidate (more than 50 percent of the vote cast), there is a later runoff election involving only the two leading candidates. The idea is to winnow the field to the two strongest candidates, and then let the whole electorate decide between them. Seems fair, and is very widely used.

Consider a case mentioned by Steven Brams (who has done lots of good work on voting). It is characterized by a table like the one above, with seventeen voters and four candidates. We'll use the same names, just to increase the confusion.

(6)	(5)	(4)	(2)
Alf	Cad	Bob	Bob
Bob	Alf	Cad	Alf
Cad	Bob	Alf	Cad

Remember that these are just preference lists—in the real election each voter would presumably vote for his first choice, and there would be no record of the voters' next preferences. So the result of this election is a tie between candidates Alf and Bob, with six votes each, while Cad is eliminated, with only five votes. There is no majority candidate, so a runoff is necessary. Since the purpose of a runoff is precisely to eliminate the least-loved candidate, and then let all the voters try again to decide between the front-runners, it is doing its job here. Assuming now that the disappointed Cad supporters move to their second choice, Alf; that would give Alf an additional five votes in the runoff, and a decisive victory over Bob. So far so good—the runoff has done its job, and Alf is the people's choice in a direct contest with Bob. He deserves the job.

But now imagine that just before the original election takes place Alf performs some act of heroism—imagine that he rescues a drowning child, or climbs a tree to save a cat—and the two voters who had originally supported Bob switch their allegiance to Alf at the last moment. *Now he loses!* In the main election he now has eight votes, still short of a majority, but Bob has fallen to four votes, and is now the one eliminated. In the runoff Alf still keeps his eight votes, but Cad picks up four more votes from the disappointed Bob voters, and is now the winner, nine to eight.

What has happened is amazing, and ought to be unacceptable if we really want the result of an election to somehow reflect the will of the people. Candidate Alf would have won, had he not attracted extra support through his heroism. It is ridiculous to have a system in which a candidate can lose an election he would have won, just because he did something praiseworthy that attracted more votes. Of course, this may not happen often, but it ought not to happen at all. Yet exactly this runoff system is everywhere. Astute politicians have learned, of course, to manipulate the weaknesses of the system to their advantage, by throwing support to a weak opponent in the early going, so he can get into the runoff and be clobbered then.

The upshot is that different systems fulfill different objectives. Winner-take-all (our system) penalizes minority views (and often majority views, as in the 1992 presidential election), while proportional representation (more common elsewhere) works against front-runners, and often leads to paralysis and indecision. Autocracy facilitates decision making, but provides few checks and balances to guard against truly dreadful decisions. Yet in a genuine emergency, effective leadership—meaning fewer cooks in the kitchen—can make the difference between survival and demise. (Even incompetent generals are better than none at all—more about that later. One reason it was easy for our Founding Fathers to make the president commander-in-chief of the armed forces was that nearly everyone trusted and revered George Washington. That state of mind has been notably missing in some recent cases.) In an economy of abundance individual freedom and maximal democracy are highly prized; in an economy of scarcity (to which the entire globe is now inexorably headed) they may be regarded as matters of secondary importance, compared to simple survival. These are all transcendentally important issues, going far beyond voting systems, and no solutions to them will be found in this simple book on decision making. But even after the question of objectives is resolved, if it ever is, a voting system designed to elicit the will of the people ought to be unambiguous, and some that are in common use are not even that.

It isn't easy to explain these issues to people—they smack of mathematics, and rational reform is a long way off. This author once tried to explain all this to a committee of distinguished engineers, in order to effect an improvement in the committee's system for choosing candidates for membership. Their eyes glazed over, and nothing was done. But the subject is genuinely important, because it is decision making at a high level.

12

Impossibility

In Chapter 10 we began to look at the problems of multiparty, multicriterion decision making (lots of options, lots of criteria, lots of voters), using the examples given by the good Reverend Dodgson as crutches. We then touched on similar problems in Chapter 11, in connection with voting systems. It is easy to wonder if these are all oddball cases, invented by the author for his own devious reasons, or if there is something deeper going on, with these problems just symptoms of a more fundamental defect.

Forty years ago, Professor Kenneth Arrow (an economist who received a Nobel Prize for the work) proved a marvelous theorem, now familiarly known as the impossibility theorem, that carries the whole subject to a higher plane. He proved that there is *no way at all, none,* to invent an unambiguous decision-making rule for multiparty, multicriterion decisions based on rankings, provided we insist on certain simple requirements (to be revealed in a moment), every one of which seems completely sensible. The theorem is far from obvious; if it were obvious, it wouldn't have taken centuries to be discovered, and wouldn't have rated a Nobel Prize. In the case in which the author tried to introduce the idea to the committee of engineers mentioned at the end of the last chapter, their response was the same as the first reaction of people who are told they have a social disease: first denial, then indifference, then an attack on the credibility of the messenger. This chapter will be devoted to the impossibility theorem, and the reader is welcome to react appropriately.

The theorem applies to a very specific but common situation. There is a collection of decision makers, called voters, or committee members, or members of the board—it doesn't matter, since the theorem is applicable to all of these. There are a number of options (three or more) that need to be ranked in some order by the group, and again we don't care what criteria, wisdom, or biases each participant brings to the table. (If there are only two options, majority voting works just fine—we need more than two before we get into trouble.) The criteria can be rational or irrational, principled or Machiavellian, wise or unwise; it only matters that each participant rank the options according to his own standards. Then the problem is simply to determine the group's ranking from the collection of individual rankings—after all, that is the essence of democracy. Some individuals can even have more votes than others—no need for real democracy here! (That's the equivalent of having a voting bloc, or members of a political party, marching in lockstep.) It is an entirely familiar situation, faced daily by nearly all decision-making groups. It applies to elections, to scholarship awards, to selection of most-valuable players, and so forth. In practice, we do this kind of thing all the time, with few complaints about the various methods, so what's the fuss?

Arrow looked for the most general method that satisfied his collection of only a few commonsense requirements. Remember, the only issue before us is how to somehow forge the individual rankings into a group ranking. We are not concerned with fairness or justice, just whether it can be done at all. We want to turn the individual rankings into a group list. Each individual brings a personal ranking list to the table, and the group ranking list leaves the table. That's all.

Here are the requirements laid down by Arrow.

- If the individuals all agree, so should the group. If everyone brings the same rankings to the table, that should be the way the group decision turns out. Unanimity should work. Who could argue with that?

- If, after the individual rankings have been used to create the group list, you then add new options, the previous rankings of the previous options should be the same as if it had been done in the other order, adding the options first and merging the lists later. That implies a certain robustness for the method—if you add some option later, and fit it in anywhere, it shouldn't affect the *relative* rankings of the ones you've already considered and ranked. Similarly for removal of an option. For example, if the group prefers spinach to cauliflower, and someone notices that the broccoli just arrived, it can be fitted into each individual's list, but that shouldn't switch the group preference to cauliflower over spinach. They may love or hate broccoli, but they haven't changed their *relative* preferences for other vegetables. The same applies if broccoli happened to be in the original list and the supply ran out, its removal shouldn't affect the ordering of spinach and cauliflower. If this weren't required of a reasonable system for synthesizing individual rankings into group rankings, any decision could be invalidated by bringing in new irrelevant options. Since no group could ever be considered to have thought of everything, no decision could ever be made.

• If the group ranking ends up with spinach preferred to cauliflower, and you add to the group another member who also prefers spinach to cauliflower (whatever else he likes or dislikes), that shouldn't switch the group preference to favoring cauliflower over spinach. Providing additional support for an option ought not to make it *less* desirable for the group. (We saw the opposite in the case of runoff voting.) Equivalently, if a participant switches his vote to spinach after it has won group preference, perhaps just to go along with the crowd, that shouldn't cost spinach its victory.

That's it, and who could disagree with any of this? Every one of these requirements for a sensible system seems eminently rational, and ought to be a requirement for any reasonable system for multiparticipant decision making.

Yet the remarkable fact that Arrow proved is that there is *no way* to devise such a decision-making system without further restrictions on the rankings provided by the individual decision makers. The proof is slightly complicated, not very, but is quite formal, and we'll pass up the chance to reproduce it here. There are many books on the subject. An even more remarkable fact (at least to this author) is that, apart from the professionals who work in this field, no one seems to care a fig about this. Committees, electorates, and boards of directors just go on about their business, untroubled by irrationality, allowing themselves to make decisions that can be manipulated by experts on parliamentary tricks.

Now it must be admitted that you have been shamefully deceived; we omitted an important point. Arrow's theorem has a loophole we didn't bother to mention. He did indeed prove what we said, that there is no method that satisfies all the requirements laid out, *but with one exception.* The exception is especially interesting, because it has troublesome practical implications. It is that all the consistency conditions can indeed be met, in all cases, *provided* that you give the authority to only one of the decision makers. In other words, consistency is obtained if there is a dictator—others can vote, but their votes don't count. Then there is no ambiguity, and rationality is restored. The historical implications can be left to the reader.

If you look for the roots of the problem, one of them was first mentioned in the writings of the Marquis de Condorcet in 1785, and is an extension of the kind of group intransitivity we mentioned at the end of Chapter 11. As the number of participants grows, and as the number of options grows, it becomes more and more likely that there are hidden loops in the ratings lists, confounding all efforts to derive a group preference from the individual preferences. There is no weighting system that can avoid this problem (other than the dictator solution).

Among the methods that most people believe can avoid ambiguity, Borda's method, briefly mentioned in Chapter 11, deserves special mention, if only because it's the one most commonly offered when this subject comes up. (People do get very defensive—no one wants to believe any of this.) We'll use the form of Borda's method in which a candidate in first place on someone's list gets one point, second place gets two points, and so forth. Then the scores are added up, and the smallest score wins. That's a method that is used everywhere. (You can do it the other way around, by giving more points to the top of a list—it doesn't matter.) It is very simple, and it is easy to know who wins. How does it run afoul of Arrow's proof—which of the axioms does it violate? And does it matter? All fair questions.

Consider an example, like those we discussed in Chapter 11, in which seven voters vote on three candidates, named, as usual, *a*, *b*, and *c*. Here are the individual ballots, with the candidates ordered as shown.

b	*b*	*c*	*a*	*b*	*c*	*b*
a	*c*	*a*	*c*	*a*	*a*	*a*
c	*a*	*b*	*b*	*c*	*b*	*c*

If we award points as specified above we find that *b* is the winner, with thirteen points, and *a* is in second place, with fourteen. In fact, *b* also has four first-place votes, a majority, so that sounds just right. Anyone would accept the results of such an election.

But now the spoiler candidate *d* enters the race at the last minute. He is a mediocre party hack—not bad, but not good, with lots of friends—and the voters are unanimous in placing him in third place, out of the (now) four candidates. They don't have the heart to rate him last—he's an old friend and throws good parties. The previous third-place candidates are all bumped down to fourth. It doesn't matter much, because they weren't going to win anyway. The table now looks like this:

b	*b*	*c*	*a*	*b*	*c*	*b*
a	*c*	*a*	*c*	*a*	*a*	*a*
d	*d*	*d*	*d*	*d*	*d*	*d*
c	*a*	*b*	*b*	*c*	*b*	*c*

If we now do the ranking as before, with Borda's method but now with rankings from one to four, the election results are different. The winner is now *a*, with fifteen points, while *b* has dropped into second place, with sixteen. So *d*, a candidate no one took very seriously, and who never came close, has switched the scores of the two top candidates, and determined the winner. That violates Arrow's second axiom, which is that once the voters have finished putting their selections in order of preference, and the final group preference is determined from the individual preferences, the introduction of a new option—a spoiler—ought not to change the order of the ones previously chosen. Of course, the new one has to fit in somewhere, perhaps even first, but an irrelevancy should not upset the *existing* order. As we said earlier, without this requirement you could never decide anything. If new irrelevancies could upset decisions already made, then all bets are truly off.

People confronted with this situation (once they are bludgeoned into believing it) often say that, oh well, this sort of thing won't happen often. In fact, the probability that there are such problems increases as the number of criteria and the number of options increase. In voting or scholarship situations we may have ten or more candidates competing, while some major industrial decisions may be founded on a hundred or more criteria (equivalent to voters). Then the sky's the limit.

Everything we have said in this chapter is based on the use of ranking schemes, or statements of preference, as they are commonly used in politics and in industry. It is possible to resolve all ambiguities by giving candidates numerical grades (as schools often do), which can then be averaged to obtain a ranking list. Then there are other problems, some of which we have touched upon, but ambiguity is not among them.

13

Protecting the Future

Decisions are easiest when the options can be directly compared. It's easy to choose between a good apple and a bad apple, harder between a good apple and a good pear, even harder between a bushel of apples and a sirloin steak, and harder still between a sirloin steak and a new pair of shoes. Between really diverse items, too different for direct comparison, there is no alternative but to rank them on some common scale, like their utilities. This isn't just academic; society makes us do it whether we like it or not, and whether we like to admit it or not, if only because we (or at least most of us) have a fixed budget and must end up paying our bills. That alone requires choices among options, based on what they are worth to us in hard cash. Of course, some things in life aren't so easy to measure in cash. There are apparently free decisions, like whether to go for a walk or take a nap, but even there one can imagine the question, "How much is it worth to you?" Money is a society's effort to reduce everything to a common measure, and get us away from trading clamshells for pottery. Given the ubiquity and popularity of money, the system seems to work. But what about comparing present money with future money? That's a new dimension.

Does it make more sense to invest in the future, or to spend what you earn as fast as it comes in? "Present mirth hath present laughter, What's to come is still unsure," said Shakespeare. The conflict is between immediate gratification of an immediate want or need (eating, for example) and promised benefits in the near or far future. Deferred gratification versus immediate gratification, if you like. Individuals, companies, and countries all face

89

this problem. Invest in schools or repair potholes; fix the roof now or save for a rainy day; work in your youth to enjoy the pleasures of old age, or the reverse? There wouldn't be so many proverbs exhorting us to prepare for the future if it weren't so un-natural.

And it *is* unnatural. If our generous genie of Chapter 9 were to announce that anyone who showed up in the village square next Tuesday would get a choice between a crisp new hundred-dollar bill and an IOU promising a hundred dollars in ten years, it's easy to figure out which option most of us would take. There is no incentive whatever to look to the future when the present is already attacking us. Besides, as Shakespeare said, the future is uncertain. (According to a famous old joke, that is an optimistic view.) Omar Khayyám wrote, "Ah, take the Cash, and let the Credit go, Nor heed the rumble of a distant Drum!" Who knows whether you'll ever collect your savings, or reap the rewards of your investment? Polls show that many people contributing to the Social Security fund today are convinced that it won't be there when they need it, in a few decades. And politicians who say they are strengthening the economy for a brighter future lose consistently to those who promise a chicken in every pot tomor-row. It doesn't matter what the winners do when elected—the promise gets them the job, memories are short, and incumbency leads to tenure.

So we're in the habit of sweetening the pot, to nudge people toward paying attention to the future. We pay interest, a return on investment, just to tempt people to defer the wants or needs they might have satisfied with their current resources. That makes it a bit more palatable to give up the use of your money; you are getting something in return. The money is being rented from you. There is no magic amount of interest that is "just right" as an incentive, but human experience seems to have settled around the range of 5 to 10 percent per year as the premium re-quired to separate people from the immediate use of their money—from immediate gratification. The interest rates vary with risk—lower rates for essentially risk-free investments, higher for speculative investments that may lead to a loss of everything, and higher still for usury, loan-sharking, and credit card balances. Higher still if the country is in deep economic trouble, and the future is even more uncertain than usual—when inflation is 100 percent per year, interest rates have to keep up. The point is simply that offering people the prospect of *more* return in the future can offset their normal and understandable reluctance to part with their possessions today. Every branch of the human race known to this author, at all times and places, has discovered this universal truth. The rates vary according to the local circumstances of time and place, but the principle stays the same.

At this point some readers may complain that the Moral Imperative to save for the future, or to invest in the welfare of one's own children and grandchildren, to say nothing of the rest of the human race, hasn't gotten a fair shake here. In short, that this author is amoral. Perhaps so, but if you think about it, all our moral imperatives are themselves local to time and place, and are simply distillations of earlier societal needs, codified so we no longer have to think about where they come from—like the multiplication table. Sometimes these lessons are collected in a body of law, sometimes in religious mandates, sometimes in various codes of ethics, and so forth, but they all, in the end, reflect the pragmatic needs of some earlier society that somehow survived. Imperatives left to us by ancient history and experience, however persuasively packaged, and however well trained we may be to obey them, fall quickly by the wayside under immediate stress. Recent human history provides far too much horrible proof of this. This is not to say that the forces aren't powerful—many of us would willingly give our lives to save our children—but to remind readers that the social forces all have their origins in our evolutionary past. Many other animals will also sacrifice themselves for the survival of their progeny, with the same drives, but without the elaborate rationalizations.

But that is a digression. The real point is that unless we improve the attractiveness of distant gratification, it doesn't stand a chance of competing with instant gratification.

It's possible to think of the interest rates needed to encourage investment either as interest on the present investment or as discounting of the future reward. If an investment of $100 now, at an annual interest rate of 5 percent, would bring (as it would with annual compounding) a windfall of $1,000 in 47 years, that could be thought of as either interest on the present investment, or as discounting the future benefit by 5 percent per year. With the second way of thinking, you would say that you want the $1,000 in 47 years, so its discounted value now is only $100, and that's what it's really worth at this time. It's the price you'd pay now for the future reward, however you think of it. Banks and insurance companies do this sort of thing as a way of life. When you pay a premium on life insurance, you are doing both at once—you are making interest-bearing investments to pay for the presently discounted value of your life. Since you are expected to die (and your heirs to collect the insurance) at some later time, there is no reason to pay full price now. And the insurance companies know very well how to discount the value of your life—that's why they employ actuaries. Sounds cold-blooded, but who ever said that insurance on your life wasn't a cold-blooded concept? Certainly you, as an individual, can hardly win that one.

It cuts both ways. Just as a distant reward isn't as attractive as a present one, and therefore costs less if you pay for it now, so a distant loss isn't as fearful as a present one. Offer people the choice between a flood tomorrow and one in fifty years, and see how many jump at the chance to get it over with. In the life insurance case above, you can think of the insurance benefits as income to your family (assuming they are your beneficiaries), to compensate them for their loss. The payment and the loss occur at about the same time, so both are discounted for the premium calculation. For most people the time horizon for the discounting of future losses ends with their own life span, or their children's or grandchildren's—for societies or countries, it may be a bit longer (although the current trend seems to be for many countries to have shorter attention spans than individuals). There is a point beyond which it makes no sense at all—who would buy a bond guaranteed to pay off magnificently in a mere thousand years? There is no case in human history in which such bonds have been sold (as far as this author knows—good hucksters can sometimes sell people awfully nutty things). And some societies and empires with exaggerated visions of their own staying power have been known to build things designed to last thousands of years. The pyramids are still there. (But read Shelley's poem "Ozymandias," which puts such aspirations in perspective.)

What has this to do with decision making? For some personal decisions that have future impact the deferral period is sufficiently short to make discounting of the future easy, but occasionally you have to match an immediate gain or loss against something so far in the future that even the usual sweeteners (or discount rates) seem to lose their relevance. Even that thought is a function of time and place. In parts of the world in which people think in terms of family dynasties, it is not unusual to make investments that will bear fruit a few generations down the line, or to maintain a family homestead or farm to which each generation adds a bit during its tenancy. There are countries in which a ninety-year mortgage on a house isn't uncommon. But that kind of long-range thinking is rare in the United States these days.

Here's a specific, and particularly egregious, case. Everyone knows (and it is even true) that sufficiently large doses of radiation can cause cancer, and that the spent fuel from nuclear power plants is radioactive. Yet, despite the almost unanimous clamor of the media, there is no evidence whatever that small exposures to radiation do any harm at all. That's a common situation—many things that are harmful in large doses are harmless in small doses. Overdoses of such a benign chemical as aspirin kill a few people each year. The number of aspirin fatalities each year has been going down, but partly because people have been substituting other well-advertised analgesics for aspirin. Small doses of aspirin are about as safe as any drug on the market. Even water is harmful in large enough doses. Anyway, the risk of radioactive exposure in small doses has motivated the Environmental Protection Agency to set a standard under which spent fuel from nuclear power plants must be isolated from human contact for ten thousand years. That's one of the most stunningly mindless government rules this author has ever seen—imagine, ten thousand years, for a country that is barely two hundred years old—but let's dig into it as an extreme example of overplaying the protection of the future.

First, what will a life be worth in ten thousand years? Regulatory activities these days seem to be settling in at a value of about a million dollars for a life—that's what juries award in cases of wrongful death, and is also the invisible line that divides government action from inaction on perceived risks (except in special cases, like coal miners and astronauts, for whom we spend far more per theoretical life saved). So let's use that estimate of the value of life, and assume that the buried material is somehow released into the environment in ten thousand years.

By then it will have decayed, and be barely radioactive, far less so than the original ore from which it was fabricated, but we'll ignore that, too—after all, the EPA doesn't seem to care about that basic fact. And we have to assume that the people who are around then won't know how to deal with radioactive materials—that they'll be much dumber than we are. So we'll assume that in ten thousand years, the released fuel will surely kill ten thousand people, at a cost of $1 million (in current money) each. That's a catastrophe worth $10 billion, in ten thousand years, against which we want to buy insurance. (To put it in perspective, that is far less than Americans now spend each and every year to buy cocaine, and far less than the projected cost of the space station.)

But we want insurance, and the only remaining question is to set the premiums according to the usual actuarial rules—in such a way that the invested money will provide the payoff at the proper time. We'll invest the money at 4 percent, another conservative estimate. It turns out that the premiums are so far below one cent per year that they are impossible to calculate. The first red cent we pay in premiums whenever we feel the urge will produce the required trust fund of $10 billion in a mere seven hundred years, with no further premiums, after which we can simply maintain the fund, interest-free, for the remaining nine thousand years. In fact, there is no way to keep the fund *below* $10 billion, if we can't invest less than one cent, unless we defer the first premium for more than nine thousand years. It is truly just plain silly to think of planning for such long periods of time. That's why it's a dumb rule—EPA can't do arithmetic.

But for more sensible periods, of importance to realistic (as opposed to government) decision making, the best procedure is to do as the insurance companies do. We should assume that resources spent now are invested, and that gains and losses in the future are discounted, all by an interest rate determined by circumstances. If any of the items involved also deteriorates with time, then its depreciated value in the future should be taken into account, *in addition to* the future discounting. Depreciation and discounting are entirely separate concepts, often confused with each other.

So the only impact of deferral on decision making is that, for all utilities and costs, good and bad, future events should be discounted to the present. If someone says he'll give you $1,000 in twenty years, don't think of it as $1,000. Discounted at 6 percent, it's worth about $300 today. One of the more widely advertised prize programs promises prizes of $1 million, but the fine print says $50,000 a year for twenty years. That's not worth $1 million. Discounted at 6 percent, it's worth about $600,000. A good prize, to be sure, but not the claimed million. Of course, the advertisers know that, but they assume that you don't.

14

Public Decisions

When people organize themselves (or are organized by others) into groups, clubs, committees, political parties, or countries, small or large, there is no way to avoid the question of how decisions are made on behalf of the group. In principle the objective should be that the decisions serve the best interests of those affected, but that principle gets more lip service than attention. It is usually far from obvious what those best interests even are; they depend on external conditions—harsh or benign, isolated or social, surrounded by enemies or friends, homogeneous or inhomogeneous, and so forth. Despite what we are taught in the schools about the superiority of the "American Way," there is no "best" form of government, suitable to all times and places, and it is plain vanity to believe that others will always be better off if they do as we do. The theme of this chapter will be that the public decision-making structure (the government) can take different forms, depending on the role it is expected to fulfill, and that, as always, decisions are more likely to turn out well if they come *after* you know what you want, not before.

More often than we would like, those who are governed have little say about *how* they are governed, and decision-making authority within a group is simply seized by a subset of individuals, or a political party, or an army, with little underlying rationale beyond a lust for power. (That lust is deeply ingrained in the human race, has a long history, and will not be magically erased by sermonizing.) Once the power is in hand, the seizure can be justified in retrospect—the winners usually rewrite history. But that's not our subject here; we want only to ask how the allocation of decision-making power (call it government, if you will) is related to the problems of a society, both real and perceived.

It is a truism that all existing societies have had survival as an overriding goal—those that haven't paid enough attention to this mundane need aren't around anymore—but the modern and affluent societies have more complex drives superimposed on that one, often losing sight of their own fragility. Corporations have different management structures from families, families from countries, tribes from nations, and committees from parliaments. In most cases, the arrangement evolves over the years or centuries as the waves of power flow back and forth, with little thought to any underlying philosophy, and little recorded rationale. There are, of course, exceptions to this overstatement, as in the writings of Plato, Aristotle, Thomas Hobbes, Jean-Jacques Rousseau, John Locke, Montesquieu, and even our own Tom Paine, but those are small creeks compared to the mighty river of human history. Even now, when starting to write this chapter, this author asked a number of his friends, some of them distinguished professors of political science, if there were any good modern books about comparative government, comparing (with substance, not slogans) different ways of organizing a society. It turned out that there were few, if any, for reasons about which we can only conjecture. (Fred Brooks, the noted computer scientist, has said that any field that needs to add the word *science* to its name probably isn't one.) There are hundreds of books on how to make democracy work better, and even more on its defects, but those are aimed at the problems of the here and now, not at the general principles. And, as mentioned earlier, the word *democracy* doesn't appear in either our Constitution or Declaration of Independence.

The historic form of government, going back to antiquity, is by a leader or king or chief, chosen by any of many criteria (size, strength, age, ferocity, birthright, sexual prowess, message from the gods, or whatever it takes to rationalize power over others), and given (or preempting) some level of authority to make decisions for the group. This pattern is ubiquitous, but not universal, in the kingdom of social animals. Groups of dogs tend to follow this pattern, but not cats. This author once saw a herd of elands in Africa, consisting of one dominant male leading his group of a few dozen females, while a herd of disenfranchised males circled the group, presumably waiting for him to get tired. Someone must know why the elands developed this pattern for survival, but it isn't obvious. Humans are not as different from other animals as we sometimes wish. Once, on a trip to France, a guide was showing an American group through a museum of Charlemagne memorabilia, and someone in the group innocently asked just how many children Charlemagne had had. The answer was that it isn't known or knowable, since he claimed the right to the first night of every bride. Whether true or not, the story called to mind the elands.

The traditional leadership form of government is often combined with some constraints on the leader—leaders tend to be capricious, and must keep their focus on the fight for group survival against both natural and unnatural enemies. After all, the facts of evolution are just as irresistible for societies as for individuals. Survival of the fittest is a definition, not a theory. Even in post-revolutionary America, with all its concerns about tyranny, the Founding Fathers found it appropriate to make the president commander-in-chief of the armed forces. (It is an ancient tradition to have the king serve as both military and political leader.) There is little room for leisurely debate if a country's existence is threatened, and leadership in a crisis, however inept (within reason), is better than no leadership at all. Our country has been, in historical fact, more the predator than the prey on this continent, so we haven't been forced to think about survival since the War of 1812. The Civil War was about partition, not survival. Since no wars since 1812 have actually threatened our survival, we've become complacent, and will one day pay the price. We have no leadership arrangement worth mentioning for the economic and social crises that bedevil us now, so they continue to fester, frustrating both those in and those out of government. And on a global level, there is no threat to human survival greater than that posed by world overpopulation—paradoxical though that may seem—and it is abundantly clear that consensus decision making is ineffective for dealing with that. Some kind of "solution" is nonetheless unavoidable, and is certain to be ugly. To say that there is no visible world leadership on that transcendental question is to understate the case. Optimists on the population problem don't measure progress in terms of a decrease in population, or even in a decrease in the rate of increase, but in terms of a decrease in the rate of increase of the rate of increase.

When a society evolves past the simple struggle for survival (or believes that it has), other values that contribute to decision making become more important. The eighteenth century brought to Western Europe and to the United States the idea of individual rights as a guiding principle of government, though the word *rights* is a slippery one indeed. The works of some of the philosophers mentioned above contain the fundamental (and, in the view of this author, unchallengeable) view that the substance of legitimate government is a trade by individuals, in which we surrender some part of our individual sovereignty in return for the benefits of coordinated response to the problems that confront a whole society. (That is called the social contract view of government. It includes giving up your "right" to plunder your neighbor's barn whenever it is convenient.) A feudal lord extracted taxes and servitude in return for cooperative protection against predators. (Remember this when we get to Lanchester's law in a couple of chapters.) Our own Constitution mentions domestic tranquility and provision for the common defense as among its primary aims. That's why the states gave up some sovereignty; they had just finished fighting the British, and it was clear that no one state could have stood by itself.

But then where did our prized individual rights come from? The Declaration of Independence declares individual rights to include "Life, Liberty, and the pursuit of Happiness," says that they are unalienable, and asserts that they came from the Creator. (So much for the separation of church and state.) The contemporaneous French Declaration of the Rights of Man lists "liberty, property, security, and resistance to oppression" as the rights to which we are entitled. (The Second Amendment to our Constitution was written with popular resistance to oppression in mind, though its original purpose seems to have been lost in the current debate over gun control, hunting, and crime.) The French gave no excuse for their particular list—it is a flat declaration, and they were apparently reluctant to rely on the Creator. Virtually all the early philosophers, the American and the French among them, included among our basic rights the right to rebel against a government deemed oppressive—that is the central theme of our own Declaration of Independence. Yet in virtually all governments founded on those principles, including ours, it is illegal to do so. So much for that right—no government that already exists likes to be overthrown. The definition of *rights* is a negotiable part of the social contract. Our Bill of Rights was not part of the original Constitution, and was added only after the Constitution had been ratified and had taken effect. (A motion to put such matters into the original version was put to a vote in the Constitutional Convention, and was defeated.)

The English Magna Carta, predating all of these recent documents by over five hundred years (1215 A.D.), was extracted by the English barons from King John, "by the grace of God, King of England, Lord of Ireland, Duke of Normandy, . . ." (Apparently his source of power was unable to protect him from his barons. Or, more likely, indifferent.) The Magna Carta has a comprehensive list of sixty-three rights, demanded by the barons, including the right of a widow to live in her husband's house for forty days after his demise. It also provides other protections for individuals, among them that "no one shall be arrested or imprisoned upon the appeal of a woman, for the death of any other than her husband." And, as a clincher, "All Counties, and Hundreds, Trethings and Wapentakes, . . . shall be at the ancient rent, without any increase. . . ." The Magna Carta is worth reading, simply because it is rich in specifics and provides a healthy perspective on the extent to which our view of the rights to which we are entitled changes profoundly with time and place. As far back as the earliest biblical times, the commandment "Thou shalt not kill" applied to thy friends and neighbors—all bets were off when dealing with tribal enemies. Especially when they had other religious predilections.

Given all that history, designed to promote humility and perspective in the reader, how do governments function as decision makers? Through all of the discussion, bear in mind Arrow's theorem of Chapter 12: there is no way to share responsibility for decisions, without ambiguity. That is pure logic, not social commentary.

Authority

This one is easy, because it's the exception to Arrow's theorem. There is no ambiguity if one person makes the decisions for all. For people living in a perilous world it has a lot going for it. The trouble, of course, is that the values that influence an authority figure's decisions may not be those of the rest of the community. History is full of examples of destructive wars fought for the pride of a monarch, as it is full of wartime leaders who maintained their domination long after the crisis had passed. People who taste power learn quickly to like it, and don't often yield it with good grace. Their decisions then reflect this adjustment of values, losing relevance to the best interests of the group. (Note the current conflict about term limits in our own Congress. Reelection jumps quickly to the top of the priority list for anyone who has once been elected.)

With a single authority, many of the theoretical problems of government are automatically resolved. Unfortunately, as was already clear to Aristotle more than two thousand years ago, the road from benign authority to tyranny is short, straight, and well trodden. Yet there are circumstances in which autocracy gives a society its best shot at survival, and it can be no accident that it was so widespread in human society for so long. Democracy as a guarantor of a society's survival has yet to demonstrate that kind of staying power, and we have already mentioned that Aristotle believed it simply could not. We'll have more to say about that subject shortly, since it hits close to home. It is decision making, so it belongs in the book.

One problem for focused authority is the inevitable transfer of power—even absolute rulers die. It is certainly not conducive to the survival of a society to have a civil war each time a monarch or chief goes to the great beyond. The traditional solution to that question is through hereditary monarchies, a practice that extends far back into antiquity, and is a simple and workable form of succession, as long as the dynasty holds out. It precludes conflict every time there is a change of the guard, and seems to work. That doesn't mean that the best-qualified person gets the job, only that the transfer can occur without bloodshed. It's the system we use in our Congress (but not in the presidency), and for exactly that reason. Of course, in the Congress succession isn't really hereditary (though there have been exceptions even to that), but the seniority system for status and committee chairmanships is the functional equivalent. As long as it is deemed acceptable by the senators and congressmen, it guarantees a relatively peaceful transfer of power when the physical and mental ravages of age force an old-timer to step down, or even die. Sometimes the change is made necessary by a lost election, but that doesn't happen very often.

So the major decision-making problem involved in government by authority is the conflict of priorities between the value system of the decision maker and that of the society. Historically, if the conflict is won by the society it is only at the price of conflict. Even King John almost immediately reneged on the terms of the Magna Carta. If you want to have decisions made clearly, quickly, and unambiguously, put someone in charge. It may not work forever, but it can work for a time. Management experts in the business world know this, as do armies. And there is plenty of historical evidence of long and stable dynasties in the ancient world.

Notice that there has been no mention of the "rights" of man in this discussion—such systems do not predispose toward individual rights.

The Common Good

In the mid–nineteenth century there was a burst of enthusiasm for the view (often associated with the name of Jeremy Bentham) that the ultimate purpose of government is somehow to assure the greatest good for the greatest number, an appealing slogan. Bentham himself believed that this was measurable—that there existed a way of measuring the total societal excess of pleasure over pain (his definition of the greatest good), so that one could make decisions with the purpose of maximizing the net pleasure/pain difference. There is, of course, enormous ambiguity, and therefore controversy, about what constitutes the common good, let alone pleasure and pain, but the view that there is *something* that can be maximized—normally not as simple as the pleasure margin—is not so far from the theme of this book. Whether it is the common good or the potential for survival or the exaltation of the best and the brightest or even the exaltation of the least fit, there remain the usual decision-making questions of objectives, measurement, and strategy. In short, implementation, without which social theory is empty.

And the doctrine of the greatest good for the greatest number sets no real standard for the amount of misery that may be imposed on a minority in support of a majority. In an extreme version, it could be argued that since medical costs for the elderly extract such a large fraction of our national income, with so little potential for pleasure or even much life extension for these same elderly, the greatest societal good could be achieved by putting them out to pasture (euphemistically). Of course, few Americans would go that far today, but in a stressful environment it might be more thinkable, even attractive. The common good is always in conflict with concern for individuals, and it doesn't help rational decision making to pretend otherwise. Besides, the common good and the common want may themselves have little to do with each other.

The problem shows up in many ways. Leniency for criminals who have been molded by miserable childhoods may be humane, but it creates a potential for later mischief that a more common-good society might not wish to tolerate. Whatever the heart-rending reason for embarking on a life of crime, habitual criminals are a problem for the rest of society. The rationalizations for their behavior don't help at all. In our schools these days, so much attention and compassion is lavished upon slow learners (*intellectually challenged* is the term that has displaced *learning disabled*) that the gifted are rarely developed to full potential, with a consequent loss to society's productivity, and therefore to all of us. And concern for the happiness and psyche of students has led to resistance to any sort of measurement of the learning progress, making it easier to ignore the appalling decline in the nation's educational standards. The thrust of education has turned against achievement, and toward preserving the self-esteem of nonachievers. If pleasure is the unvarnished objective, that's fine. You don't actually have to accomplish anything to feel pleasure and pride, you just have to *think* you have. But for the prospects of the society, whose long-term pleasure margin depends vitally on real achievement, that view is deadly.

So the ancient conflict between the good of the individual and the good of the society molds the decision-making procedures. The founders of our system of government (and many others) tried to devise a system of representation that steered clear of Aristotle's ochlocracy, yet provided adequate protection against the abuse of individuals in the name of the common good. So we can stand on a street corner and denounce the president, but can't (in the classic example) yell "Fire!" in a crowded auditorium. We can openly welcome a riot, but we cannot incite a riot. It sometimes gets silly—there are cases in which a person is allowed to harass another at the office, but not at home, or only from a distance of more than twenty yards. We are guaranteed free speech, but the line between spirited criticism and slander is understood only by lawyers, and then only by specialists. An English publisher recently sued an American learned society that had published data showing that very few people actually read and used the publisher's output. (The aggrieved publisher lost, because the statement was true. Sometimes that actually matters.)

Those may seem trivial examples, but it is very difficult to maintain a balance between the individual good and the common good—the line is fuzzy. And on top of all that, it isn't possible to protect the common good by making decisions based entirely on the views of those whose good is being protected. The original purpose of democracy was to prevent certain specific kinds of evil, not to do good.

A hundred years ago, in an infamous event, a bill was introduced into the Indiana Legislature that would have certified a particularly silly, and wildly wrong, value of pi (π), the ratio of the circumference of a circle to its diameter, as the value to be used in Indiana. (The bill's sponsors also proposed to license the use of that value to others, and the legislative debate was full of discussion of the profits it would bring to Indiana.) Had that bill passed (it did pass on first reading, but wiser heads caught on to what was happening, and succeeded in blocking it), and had it been enforced, nothing round would have worked in Indiana. Voting is no way to answer technical questions, though it may give pleasure to the voters. This author, a physicist, would hate to see the validity of the theory of relativity put to a vote. If that sounds elitist, it should. It is an unpopular but sound principle that you ought to know something about a subject before you earn the right to express an opinion about it. The schools now teach the opposite—that your view is as "valid" as anyone else's, no matter how little you know. That not only encourages self-esteem, it rewards sloth.

It is hard to make the point more forcefully than did James Madison, in the tenth of the Federalist papers, the essays written by him, John Jay, and Alexander Hamilton, to persuade the citizens of New York to ratify the proposed Constitution.

> From this view of the subject it may be concluded that a pure democracy, by which I mean a society consisting of a small number of citizens, who assemble and administer the government in person, can admit of no cure for the mischiefs of faction. A common passion or interest will, in almost every case, be felt by a majority of the whole; a communication and concert result from the form of government itself; and there is nothing to check the inducements to sacrifice the weaker party or an obnoxious individual. Hence it is that such democracies have ever been spectacles of turbulence and contention; have ever been found incompatible with personal security or the rights of property; and have in general been as short in their lives as they have been violent in their deaths. Theoretic politicians, who have patronized this species of government, have erroneously supposed that by reducing mankind to a perfect equality in their political rights, they would, at the same time, be perfectly equalized and assimilated in their possessions, their opinions, and their passions.

What Madison could not have foreseen was the development of mass communication, which binds large numbers of people together, and provides them all with the same information (and misinformation), making it possible for millions to behave like the small groups he had in mind.

In summary, the common good as a standard for decision making sounds virtuous, but is not simple, not easily implementable, and certainly not universally applicable.

The Moral Imperative

The greatest good for the greatest number is pragmatically appealing, in that a government that reflects that objective as its guiding principle is likely to be well regarded by a large number of people—the recipients of the goodness. But the extreme version would lead to the quiet disposal of nonproductive members of society, and most of us would find that morally repugnant. So morality has entered the discussion.

Most of us would also regard it morally objectionable to attack someone weaker than we are, and in fact defense of the defenseless is one of our basic moral imperatives. Yet try to guess whether we would even be here if our ancestors specialized in fighting only folks stronger than they. Not likely, and they didn't. Most of us were indignant a few years ago when Saddam Hussein of Iraq attacked defenseless Kuwait, as he had been threatening to do for years. Yet he was doing what had long been customary in that part of the world. And the struggle between the American Indians and the Eastern invaders was hardly an equal struggle—its ultimate outcome was predictable. During our few centuries of history we've taken large chunks of our neighbors' territory. Our own hands are not so clean.

So support of the weak is a luxury, less often honored under stress than our training suggests it should be. Yet many (probably most) of us believe that it is as close to a real moral imperative as one can get. It is a major thesis of the New Testament, though not of many other repositories of religious doctrine. It is, however, an underlying theme of the Code of Hammurabi, the remarkable compendium of Babylonian law that predated even the Old Testament by more than a millennium (eighteenth century B.C.), and itself rested on still older bodies of law. Protection of the weak has a history as a moral imperative.

Yet in the excerpt from the Federalist papers, quoted above, we found Madison arguing that it is impossible to protect the weak within a democratic form of government, because a majority with power will find it irresistible to sacrifice the welfare of a weak minority (or an obnoxious individual, as he put it) to the passions of the majority. He was in effect saying that democracy is incompatible with morality. All through the debate in the Constitutional Convention, and in the later Federalist papers, there is a recurrent theme that aspirations to democracy must yield to the moral imperative of preserving individual rights—they are opposing forces. That is decision making at a high level; the contesting values are clearly laid out, and a compromise—a representative republic, not a democracy—was judged most likely to assure the reasonable welfare of the people, while preserving their security. The moral imperative was to preserve the rights given to the people by the Creator, as long as it didn't threaten the integrity of the Union. It's not clear who spoke to the Creator about which comes first.

Taxation without Representation

Taxation and punishment for aberrant behavior are the greatest powers of a government, and their design reflects the values of that government. All American schoolchildren learn that King George was taxing the tea imported by the American colonists (as much to make a point as to collect revenue), and that a band of angry Bostonians dumped a batch of it overboard in Boston harbor, two years before full-fledged rebellion against English rule broke out. (The Bostonians weren't quite as brave as we make them out to be in our legend—they tried to pin the blame elsewhere by disguising themselves as Indians.) But the point that a tax ought to be for the benefit of the taxed is consistent with the social contract theory of government, and the tea tax was clearly for the sole benefit of King George. The Magna Carta itself was a response to excessive taxation of the barons by King John, and resentment of taxation is a steady theme throughout history, as far back as there are any records at all.

A tax is not a direct payment for goods and services, to be paid voluntarily, and only when the benefits it buys are worth the price—like the price of cheese. It is mandatory, not paid at the pleasure or whim of the taxpayer, and is spent for things the taxpayer may not consciously want or need—like the emperor's clothes and carriage. Yet the real benefits of some necessary government services may not be immediately apparent to the taxpayer, especially when they are complex, or remote in space and time. Countries that are at peace are notoriously loath to spend good money on military preparedness; people are unwilling to support scientific research whose possible payoff is conjectural, esoteric, and in the future; nowadays, though everyone supports the concept of a fine education for the young, bond issues to support that education are routinely defeated at the polls. Yet potholes in the roads get filled, because they are evident nuisances in the here and now, both to those who will pay for the repairs, and to those who won't.

While the slogan "Taxation without Representation Is Tyranny" is widely known, and is treated as axiomatic in the schools, the decisions of tyrants on how to use taxes aren't always bad for the community of taxpayers, in the long run. Even a tyrant wants his country to survive, and his methods may sometimes be devious. A representative system like ours is supposed to strike a balance by placing an extra layer between the taxpayer's perceived need for visible returns on his taxes, and the government's need for support of those communal obligations for which a government is formed, and whose benefits may not be entirely obvious. No one knows how to make the government directly responsible to the taxpayers, while still using taxes for the common good even when the taxpayers may not be quite on board. The conundrum frustrates virtually all modern democratic governments. The dilemma is far worse in an era of mass communication, in which the complexity of many of the problems simply exceeds the taxpayers' individual capabilities (to say nothing of the legislators') to make informed judgments, and the media of communication reduce all subjects to caricatures and sound bites. Informed choice then becomes a pipe dream. (Perhaps it is heresy to say that, but honesty requires that it be said.) The solution usually mentioned when this subject comes up in polite company is that we must always strive for an educated citizenry. But we can't all be experts on everything, and it is another pipe dream to believe that we will. Besides, half the people have less than average education and intelligence, and that will always be true. It is a truism.

Representation without Taxation

But that problem is nothing compared to its converse, representation without taxation. That is the Achilles' heel of modern Western democracies, and may yet consign them to the good-idea-that-almost-worked junk heap of history. It strikes at the first principle of effective decision making: that the decision maker must have a stake in both the costs and benefits of a decision. Without that, there is no compelling incentive to make responsible decisions, and failure is both inevitable and predictable. It is impossible to overstate the importance of this subject.

The original Founding Fathers knew this, and left the question of voting rights in the hands of the states, deliberately not following the ancient tradition of letting only property owners vote. There was some interesting discussion on this point in the Constitutional Convention, in which one delegate, arguing for a property requirement, commented that if a person wanted to vote badly enough, he had only to buy some property. That view did not prevail, but it is clear that there was concern about giving fiscal authority, however remotely exercised, to voters without fiscal responsibility. The delegates knew perfectly well (as many of our current politicians have conveniently forgotten) that it is too much to expect people to be prudent in the use of other people's resources.

Two hundred years later we have come nearly all the way down that particular primrose path. About 60 percent of the federal income taxes paid to the Internal Revenue Service comes from 10 percent of the taxpayers. And there are even more voters than there are taxpayers, so ultimate decision-making authority on the expenditure of public funds in our country resides overwhelmingly in the hands of those who will not pay for the decisions they make. That paves the way for the enormous (and growing) national debt, the equally enormous deficit with which our government works each year (an option denied us as individuals), and the unstoppable growth in so-called entitlement programs. When the beneficiaries of the programs are not the payers, what could be more natural? Within our system nothing can be done about it, since a politician who promises us more benefits, paid for by anonymous others, has an edge over one who asks us to make hard choices among desirable objectives— something we do every day in our private lives. Thus, in the author's home state, California, the citizens were delighted to pass an initiative requiring insurance companies to refund 20 percent of the premiums collected—there are far more premium payers than insurance companies, so the merits of the case hardly matter. In some notorious parts of the state, voters are delighted to institute stringent rent controls—there are far more renters than landlords, so the merits of the case hardly matter. In India, the largest democracy in the world, at least half the voters are illiterate, yet they determine government policy on the most complex and challenging matters. No one dares suggest literacy tests for voting in our own country. And so forth.

The basic ailment afflicts more than the use of taxes; it affects all matters in which the unaffected or uninformed are the decision makers for all of us. A particularly visible example in the United States is in the increasing regulatory role of government. As the country becomes more urbanized, one finds the majority urban electorate more and more willing to impose burdens on what is left of rural life. The fifty-five-mile-per-hour speed limit might conceivably make some sense in the more crowded parts of the country, but was mandated for all, and was widely ignored until its repeal in 1995. (It lasted twenty years.) The passionate anti-gun legislation is primarily aimed at the problems of the big cities, but is jammed down the throats of rural America, which is accustomed to being armed, and for the most part comfortable with the fact. We are increasingly willing to regulate the way in which other people live their lives, if it is done at no cost to most of us. In California twenty-five proposed amendments to the state constitution have been put before the electorate, on a take-it-or-leave-it basis, with no possibility of negotiation or fine-tuning, but with massive, often grossly misleading, publicity campaigns. Selling a constitutional amendment in California is treated very much like selling pain relievers or breakfast cereal. It has been learned that if a proposal doesn't raise general taxes, is well packaged, and promises to hurt only a minority of the people, it has a decent chance of passing. Once adopted, such an amendment becomes part of the state constitution, changeable only through another statewide vote of the electorate. Of the twenty-five proposed amendments, about a third have passed. Whatever can be said about the unwieldy legislative process, it does allow for debate and appropriate modification of flaws in proposed legislation. And legislation, unlike constitutional amendments, is subject to later adjustment if it has unexpected effects.

Several Western democracies are further down this particular road than we, and are currently in deep political and economic trouble. The process violates the first principle of decision making, by disconnecting the costs from the benefits, which makes decisions based on a balance between them impossible. The Founding Fathers put their faith in representative government, but obviously couldn't foresee the technical advances that made possible an era of instant mass communication. This author blanches at the idea of a referendum to validate the multiplication table—we have already lost the battle to require that children learn it.

Later we will have a chapter devoted to a related subject: decision making in the judicial system. That will include the painful question of juries deliberately chosen to have no interest in the subject at hand, and often no knowledge about it either.

And, of course, our federal budget is well over a trillion dollars a year, and we have no requirement that any member of Congress (or the president, for that matter) have any experience in or knowledge about financial management. Or indeed anything at all. Nor do the few candidates who flaunt their economic expertise find it an effective selling point.

Complexity

The knowledge and experience needed to do their jobs are increasingly important for our lawmakers and other public servants, as our society becomes more complex and harder to understand, and as the consequences of public decisions become less obvious. We've devoted nearly all of this chapter to the objectives of public decisions—who decides what and with which and for the benefit of whom—but there is a dimension of social problems in which there is honest-to-golly uncertainty, and for which the decision-making person or body may simply lack the capability to make reasoned decisions. Even with all the goodwill in the world.

For technical and economic matters this is nearly always the case these days. It was different when the country was first organized—we were principally farmers and small shopkeepers, science and technology played bit roles, and central management of the national economy on a national scale was an idea for the distant future. The problems that political decision makers had to confront were closer to their own experiences and expertise, and were more limited in scope. They may have made mistakes, but they at least thought they knew what they were doing, most of the time. Uncertainty as a way of life was not the norm. And there is an innate conflict between the needs of a decision maker for decisiveness—decisions simply *must* be made—and the limited tools and expertise available to guide the decisions. All the other problems of public decision making are simply laid over this new one.

For example, the Congress must often decide whether to raise or lower taxes (the latter on rare occasions), amid conflicting and passionate views held by competent economists about the ultimate effect on the national economy—or, too often, amid uncertainty about the effect on the next election. We see the stock market indices crashing because there is good news about the economy—or sometimes zooming, depending on whether the change was within expectations. And whose expectations? These seemingly contradictory effects come from genuine uncertainties, and it is not for nothing that economics has been called the dismal science. But decisions must still be made.

It is even worse for technical matters, if only because most lawmakers think themselves experts on law and economics, but few think of themselves as competent scientists or engineers. (One even sees an inexcusable flaunting of ignorance, "I don't know any mathematics," said with pride.) Yet public decisions involving technical uncertainty can be important, and mathematics is the language of both technology and economics. (We won't belabor these points here, because we've already written a whole book about them.) As of this writing the Department of Energy has squandered tens of billions of dollars (with hundreds of billions more to come) on utterly inept schemes to accomplish the impossible in environmental restoration. The fact that an objective is worthy does not excuse ineptitude in pursuing it—or even in deciding whether to pursue it.

In such matters it is customary to convene panels of scientists or economists, who, given the nature of the problems, produce heavily hedged reports that are of little use to the officials who really need to be led to decisions. The hard work in making decisions always comes (as we have emphasized throughout the book) *after* the facts are in hand. Scientists usually say that their job is to supply the facts, leaving the decisions to the decision makers, but the decision makers are seeking help in making a decision; encyclopedic knowledge is not their goal. Facts are of secondary importance, and uncertainty, however real, is viewed as weakness, and almost subversive. Thus, former Senator Edmund Muskie was quoted as saying that the nation needed more one-armed scientists, so they couldn't respond to technical questions by saying that on the one hand this may be true, and on the other hand that.

Uncertainty has actually made some inroads in our society in recent decades, if only in weather forecasting. Hardly anyone now complains if the meteorologist says that there is a 30% chance of rain tomorrow. People go on planning their picnics with that in mind, rejoicing if it doesn't rain, complaining if it does, but rarely blaming the forecaster for not being more precise. They somehow know that it is hard to predict the weather.

But if the price is higher people are less forgiving, and require certainty, real or imagined. We ask if a building is safe, not the probability that it will fall down. We ask if AIDS can be transmitted through a kiss, not what the probability is—and we don't accept "very unlikely" as an answer. The political process, as we see it in the United States, is intolerant of uncertainty, and thereby forces politicians (and some experts) to lie, simply to be heard. The advantage goes to the official or politician who is sure of himself, even when wrong. When we reward dishonesty, we all pay the price. If not now, later.

As this is being written there has just been a little-noted event in Japan that illustrates this dilemma very well. Japan, as most of us know, is in a seismically active part of the world—the islands owe their very existence to seismic forces. And earthquakes can cause widespread damage, so most countries in seismic regions are working hard to improve the science of earthquake prediction. If timely warning can be provided, steps can be taken to limit the potential damage of an earthquake, if only through preparedness exercises. So the Japanese government has had an earthquake advisory committee, whose job has been to provide as much advance warning of impending earthquakes as possible. No one knows how to predict an earthquake precisely—it is currently a dream to believe one will be able to say there will be a Richter magnitude 7.0 earthquake on Thursday at noon. So the chairman of the committee has been arguing for years that the report should be couched in probabilistic terms (like a weather forecast), so one could simply say that there is a 30% chance of an earthquake in the next month. The government officials have rejected the argument, because they need to make decisions about what actions to take, if any, in the here and now. They want to be told whether or not there will be an earthquake, not its probability. Their need is real, so the fact that it is impossible to do this honestly in the current state of the science has no relevance to their problem. The chairman of that committee has just resigned in protest. No other members followed.

This author has a friend who was a high official in NASA during the glory years of the Apollo project, and the friend has said that he had no interest in the probability of a successful launch. He couldn't go to an astronaut and say that the launch was on because "you have an 80% chance of living through it," nor could he go to the president and say the launch was scrubbed because there was a 20% chance of failure. Neither would understand. So for years NASA faked the numbers, speaking and acting as if there were no risk at all, and the top management eventually came to believe that it was true. We all paid that price in 1986 with the *Challenger* disaster. Even after that event, NASA was arguing that the chance of failure was negligible—the Feynman addendum to the Rogers Committee report on the accident is still good reading.

We haven't touched the really hard questions of global warming, the evident failure of our educational system, the economic future of our country, the security of the country in an increasingly hostile world, and so forth. These are hard problems, and require the best of us, but instead they get sound bites. This author is a supporter of at least minimal literacy requirements for voting—having illiterate people vote may seem perfect democracy, but it leads to bad decisions—and he has been called many unflattering names as a result. But unless we bring some skills to the public decision-making process we will make terrible and costly mistakes. It is not a simple world we live in, and our survival as a nation or society is not guaranteed by any natural law.

15

Apportionment

One of the compromises that went into the Constitution of the United States provided for a bicameral Congress, a Senate with equal numbers of senators for each state and a House of Representatives apportioned according to the populations of the various states. The original House had sixty-five members, with each state's representation specified in the Constitution itself. By the time of the first census in 1790 the country's population was just under 4 million people, so one representative acted for about sixty thousand citizens. The Constitution doesn't bother to specify how large the House should be (except for the first one), but does set an upper limit: there shall be no more than one representative for each thirty thousand people. Other than that, there is no inkling of how the membership in the House is to be parceled out to the states, given their populations. This chapter is devoted to that arcane subject. It is government decision making at work.

Much of the debate in the 1787 Constitutional Convention was about the division of power between the large states and the small states. There were inevitable conflicts. Though it was in everyone's interest to form a union stronger than the 1781 Confederation, the smaller states were nervous (with good reason) about sharing their sovereignty with their big sisters. And the larger states were nervous (again with good reason) about the more numerous smaller ones taking control. So the delegates bargained away, and finally reached a compromise acceptable to both: a Senate with two senators from each state, whatever its size, and a House of Representatives with membership determined according to the state populations, but with a minimum of one representative for each state. The original Constitution further insulated the Senate from the population by specifying that senators were to be chosen by the state legislature, not directly by the people of the state. That was later changed by the Seventeenth Amendment, but not until 1913, well over a century later. The original arrangement provides some insight into the extent to which the Founding Fathers trusted ordinary people to govern themselves. They cherished freedom, but were very concerned about the pitfalls of popular government. Lincoln spoke in the Gettysburg Address, nearly a century later, about government of, by, and for the people, but the Founding Fathers had hedged the middle preposition.

The main issue before the Convention was to find a division of power and decision-making authority that made it possible for the government to function, and to somehow combine the forces of the various states where necessary for the common good (like fighting a common enemy), while still preserving their identities and their local sovereignty for other matters. Human rights guarantees were added within a few years, by amendment to the original Constitution. Among the six purposes cited in the Preamble to the Constitution, provisions for the general welfare and the blessings of liberty are listed fifth and sixth. The formation of "a more perfect" union, establishment of justice, domestic tranquility, and provision for the common defense—these come first. That's the way it was in those days.

Though most of us have never heard of apportionment, the importance attached to it by politicians can be measured by the rhetoric they have poured forth on the subject over the years. As one measure, the Constitution became effective in March of 1789, and by September of the same year the first Congress had proposed twelve amendments, of which the first two were never ratified. (The other ten are now known as the Bill of Rights.) Of the two that were proposed in the very same starting package, but not ratified, one was an effort to define more specifically how apportionment should be carried out after each census. That was a top priority for the Congress. The other would have prohibited Congress from giving itself a pay raise that would be effective before the next election. Even in those first days, that was a touchy issue. Neither of these proposed amendments survived the political process, but the problems they were meant to address live on to this day. The Constitution still leaves apportionment to the politicians most affected by it, in clear conflict with common sense, and congressional salaries are still left in the hands of the beneficiaries, again in clear conflict with common sense. Two hundred years, and no progress.

The first veto ever by a president of the United States occurred a few years later, when President George Washington vetoed the apportionment law that Congress had passed after the 1790 census results were in, deeming it inequitable. The effort to override his veto, again a first for the country, was unsuccessful. Apportionment is hardly a new subject. The outcome of that particular squabble in 1792 was to fix the size of the House at a member for each thirty-three thousand constituents, and to simply round off the fractions—you can't have fractional representatives, though it sometimes seems that way. The House was then slightly smaller than its maximum constitutional size.

Well, the population has grown since then, and is now more than sixty times as large as it was in 1790, very roughly doubling each generation, so if the House of Representatives were apportioned now at the maximum rate specified in the Constitution, or even at the slightly lower level specified by the 1792 law, it would have nearly ten thousand members. We may think we have confusion and gridlock now, but imagine what that would be like! The representatives would have to meet in a sports stadium—Madison Square Garden in New York or the Omni in Atlanta would do nicely, with a bit of room for a small spectator gallery. One could even imagine cheerleaders for the various parties romping up and down the sidelines. So to abort this trend the size of the House was frozen in 1910 (by Congress) to its present size of 435 members, providing by now, on the average, one representative for well over a half-million people. The 1990 census found three states whose entire populations were smaller than the size of an "average" congressional district.

The question of just *how* to apportion representatives was of special importance to the very smallest states. The purpose of the census every ten years is to determine the population of the country and of the several states, which then makes it possible to determine the average size of a congressional district. We then try to divide the 435 representatives equitably among the states.

But with congressional districts averaging over a half-million people, it would be an amazing coincidence if each state had a population that could be evenly divided into districts of that size. So it is not immediately obvious how to make the cut. Therein lies the decision-making problem. It is a public problem, not yielding to the simple analytic methods we talked about earlier, and involving lots of conflicts of interest. What became clear in the early years of this century was that it is pointless to expect each new Congress, after a census, to come to an agreement on how to divide the spoils. They care too much. After the census of 1920 the Congress was so divided that they couldn't agree on any reapportionment bill at all, so the 1910 apportionment continued through the 1920s. It could have gone on forever.

There are now (based on the 1990 census) seven states with only one representative, and six others with only two. So thirteen states, holding a fourth of the membership of the Senate, control less than a twentieth of the membership of the House. And it matters to the small states—the largest state (California, at this writing) would hardly notice an addition of one representative to its delegation of fifty-two (it picked up seven in 1990), while Wyoming (the least populous state) and six others would double their delegations if they got just one more. In the House, California alone can outvote the combined representatives from twenty-one states, nearly half the states of the union.

Other than specifying the minimum size of an average constituency the Constitution is completely silent on the question of apportionment. It does require that the size of the delegation be governed by a state's population, and specifies that the representatives be chosen by the people (though not how). It also says nothing about how the representatives are to be apportioned to the citizens *within* a state; those constraints have come much later, in a civil rights context, through innovative Supreme Court reinterpretations of the Constitution.

So what are the options? To make the arithmetic easy let's take an extreme case, a fictitious country that has only two states, Able and Unable, with populations of 15,000 and 48,000 respectively, and a Congress fixed at six seats. (Obviously, we've cooked our numbers carefully, to make a point.) Since the law in this imaginary country is the same as in ours—each state gets at least one seat—it seems pretty obvious that of the first five seats one should go to Able and four to Unable. Then the representative from Able will represent 15,000 citizens, while each representative from Unable will represent 12,000. You can't take away Able's guaranteed minimum of one, while giving it two representatives would mean that each of those would represent 7,500 people, leaving the remaining three Unable representatives each representing 16,000. That would be a pretty gross inequity, so the fairest disposition of the first five seats is pretty clear.

But what about the sixth seat? To whom should it go? If you give it to Able, its representatives will again be down to a constituency of 7,500 each, against Unable's 12,000, while if you give it to Unable, they will be down to districts of 9,600, compared to Able's original 15,000. What to do?

Well, there are several options, of which we'll mention only two. One goes by the fancy name of the method of the harmonic mean, which simply means that you must try to equalize the sizes of the districts in the two states, as best you can. If you give the sixth seat to Able, the district sizes will be 7,500 and 12,000, differing by 4,500; if you give it to Unable, the sizes will be 15,000 and 9,600, differing by 5,400. So the nod would go to Able, the smaller state, if you simply try to bring the sizes of congressional districts as close together as possible.

But wait, say the unhappy Unable politicians; there is a better way to do this. If you give the seat to Able, then each thousand people in its population will have a 0.133 share of a congressman, while each thousand of our people will have only a 0.083 share, which hardly seems fair. If you give the seat to us, their people will have 0.0667 congressmen per thousand, while our citizens will have 0.1042 per thousand. That discrepancy is only 0.0375, while the other way it would be 0.050, much larger. So, given the principle that each citizen should have the same representation in Congress, as close as it is possible to get that, we in Unable should get the sixth seat. (That method is known by the classy name of the method of major fractions, and was used in the early history of our country.)

So there is the problem: if you want to make the districts as close as possible to the same size, the seat goes to Able, but if you want to give each citizen equal representation in the Congress, as far as possible, then Unable should get the seat. The method of the harmonic mean favors small states, while the method of major fractions favors large states. And there are other methods with even more tilt. No wonder politicians have been fighting about this since the beginning. Someone's ox is going to be gored. And the Constitution (both in this fictitious country and in our real one) provides no help at all. In our fictitious country, Able's representation in the House can be either a third or a sixth, with no difference in population, just according to the apportionment rule chosen. Either rule would be consistent with the Constitution, *and* the politicians get to choose which they like best.

We've admittedly made up numbers that will lead to the dilemma we sought, but with the real numbers in the United States, reapportionment after each census typically leaves a few states at the borderline between getting an extra representative and not getting one, just like Able and Unable. For them the final outcome depends on the method used, and it makes a big difference. And remember, besides the influence of the delegation size on national legislation, the composition of the Electoral College depends on the number of representatives allocated to each state.

So what is a country to do, when *somebody* is bound to end up feeling underrepresented? And why didn't the framers of the Constitution tell us how to do it? Can it be that, despite their otherwise splendid educations, mathematics wasn't their strong point? Remember, Benjamin Franklin was there, but he was pretty old by then, and was a scientist, not a mathematician.

Well, this isn't a clear-cut mathematical problem, but is again a decision-making problem whose resolution depends on what you'd like to achieve. If you want to favor the small states, go for the harmonic mean. If you like the large states, major fractions are for you. That's why the issue can't be resolved by pure reason. It is necessary for Congress to come to an agreement by negotiation and compromise; logic is of little use.

On top of that, some of the methods we haven't mentioned suffer from what the politicians call paradoxes—not the same use of the word that we encountered in Chapter 10. To a politician, a paradox reflects an unwanted or unpalatable consequence of a procedure, not an apparent contradiction. When mathematics works in unexpected ways—unexpected by a politician—it is called a paradox. The two that bedeviled earlier efforts to devise apportionment systems were the so-called Alabama paradox and the population paradox. In a nutshell, the Alabama paradox afflicts an apportionment scheme if it is possible for a state's delegation to decrease when the size of the House increases, and it is then reapportioned. (It once nearly happened to Alabama.) The population paradox occurs when an increase in total population can result in a decrease in the size of the House. (Neither of these is a real paradox, but each can decrease the number of representatives, and is therefore unacceptable to representatives, some of whom might have to retire.) The population paradox is now avoided by fixing the size of the House at 435, so it can't shrink, the Alabama paradox by considering only apportionment methods that are immune to it.

So in 1941 the Congress decreed that the method to be used would be the "method of equal proportions," a vaguely descriptive name that probably doesn't mean much to anyone, but, when combined with a House of fixed size, avoids all so-called paradoxes, while not egregiously favoring either large or small states. With this method, you can go about it as follows: Use the results of each census to make a first cut at the number of representatives to be allocated to each state, according to its population. Then take the result of that preliminary allocation and adjust it by comparing the size of each state's delegation with that of each other state, according to still another peculiar rule. The ratio of the population to the number of delegates is first calculated for each of the two states to be compared, to find out the average size of a proposed congressional district, for each. Then the *ratio* of the larger to the smaller value is computed, providing a number larger than one, as a measure of how much larger the big district is than the small one. (The methods we described above took the difference of district sizes in the two states and the difference of voter representations as the criteria; this method takes the ratio.) If the ratio can be decreased (brought closer to equity) by transferring a delegate from the overrepresented state to the other, then it should be done. When it is no longer possible to reduce this ratio by transferring delegates among states, the process is complete and the apportionment has been accomplished.

That is the law, and the rationale is simply that, among the five most promising methods that have been suggested over the years, each of which *could* be used, it is in the middle in terms of preference for large or small states. That is the *only* open reason for choosing this method. The choice is a political compromise, just as was much of the original Constitution, so it should not be analyzed in terms of principles or mathematical logic.

In fact, it isn't necessary to go through this elaborate procedure to implement the method. It is easy to show (trust the author) that all that is necessary is to calculate, for each state, the average size of a congressional district for each possible number of representatives, and then rank the states in order, using as the ranking index the *product* of the size of a proposed district and its size if the delegation were increased by one. This can be done for all proposed sizes of the delegation. Then all that is necessary is to put the states and their proposed representations in order, and assign representatives until the total adds up to 435. Sounds complicated, but isn't—especially in the computer age.

How would the approved method apply to the hypothetical case above? The larger state, Unable, would get the nod by a tiny margin. That's the way the cookie crumbles.

That's the current rule, in place for the last fourth of our history as a nation. If the larger or smaller states ever got sufficient control of the process to change the law in their favor, there is nothing to bar the way. And there is no historical reason to believe they wouldn't jump at the opportunity. In this author's home state, and in many others in our country and in our history, the party in control of the state legislature at the time of reapportionment doesn't hesitate for a moment to take care of its own interests, one way or another. It is an instability against which the Founding Fathers provided no protection.

In the real world, if the (completely arbitrary) limit on the size of the House of Representatives had been set at 436 instead of 435 in 1910, then at the time of the 1990 census the next state in line for a seat would have been Massachusetts, with a small but clear lead over the next contender, New Jersey. New York comes next, well behind the leaders. (In this case the word *leader* means the first state to have missed the boat.) Massachusetts would have gone from ten seats to eleven, a nontrivial 10 percent increase in representation, and an additional vote in the Electoral College. On the other hand, if the apportionment system in use for the first part of this century had been used instead of the present system, Massachusetts would have gotten its additional seat anyway, at the expense of Oklahoma. No one likes to just miss the cut, which is why this obscure decision-making problem has preoccupied politicians for so long.

16

War:
Lanchester's Law

Given the importance of warfare in recorded human history (and doubtless long before history began to be recorded) it is surprising how little systematic attention has been paid to the search for fundamental strategic and tactical principles, compared to the effort expended on the development of new combat weapons. Of course, there are the classic principles of Sun Tzu, twenty-five hundred years ago, the maxims of Napoleon, almost three hundred years ago, and even more recent doctrines of Clausewitz, to say nothing of slogans and sound bites like "Take the High Ground," "Get There Fustest with the Mostest," and "Divide and Conquer," all of which are useful slogans in certain kinds of warfare. But they are still just slogans. It is remarkable how little *quantitative* thinking has been published on even these sloganized subjects. Qualitative innovations in both strategy and tactics occur from time to time, often with the adjustment of unusually gifted commanders to new weapons—from the introduction of the horse into combat in the first millennium B.C., through the use of the longbow in the early second millennium A.D., and more recently the strategy of deterrence, which came with nuclear weapons. And the arrival of the computer age has spawned a cottage industry in battlefield simulation and realistic war games, which are extensively used for the training of military commanders. Despite all that, general principles for decision making in wartime are hard to find. And if ever there were a place where it is costly to learn your job through trial and error, it is the battlefield.

Yet tactical decisions on a field of battle are just as much subjects for mental discipline (which is the heart of decision theory) as are all the other applications of decision making in this book. When confronted by a thinking adversary, the subject belongs to the theory of games, which makes it less transparent, but there can also be cases in which the opponent's behavior can be well enough understood, or sufficiently irrelevant, to make the decisions effectively individual matters. Then simpler methods can be helpful.

One example of the application of formal discipline to the study of battle tactics was made by an English engineer named Frederick Lanchester, one of the pioneers in the early histories of aviation and automobiles, who based his theory on a study of air battles in World War I. His excellent and insightful work is familiar to only a small fraction of modern military officers—it is mentioned in the curricula of the military academies, but is not deemed very important. If we are sufficiently cynical, we'll soon see a possible reason.

Lanchester considered a hypothetical (of course, vastly oversimplified) model of combat, in which opposing forces were simply shooting at each other, with no particular advantage in accuracy or other human or weapon characteristics on either side. (World War I, like many earlier and more recent wars, had plenty of examples of such mindless engagements.) His crucial insight was that your own firepower in such an encounter is proportional to the number of units you have, whether they are troops, ships, or aircraft, while the number of targets you present to the enemy is also proportional to the number of your units. Therefore your effectiveness depends twice on your numbers: once by increasing your own firing rate, and the other by diluting the enemy fire. The fundamental assumption is that each side is shooting at the other, with some probability, however low, of scoring a hit. (If they are shooting wildly into the darkness—a practice that military folks dignify with the long-winded expression "harassment and interdiction fire"—things are different.) In the end, and it's not hard to work out mathematically, two important consequences emerge.

The first consequence is that the strength of your forces is measured by the *square* of your number of units, not just the number, so outnumbering the enemy is a greater advantage than you might have thought. Three times the number of units (troops, airplanes, ships, tanks, etc.) leads to nine times the effectiveness. In the movies and on television the good guys (the handsome and rugged-looking actors) regularly beat up gangs of a half-dozen or more bad guys, but don't count on it in real life. The square law depends on everyone fighting at once—sometimes in the movies the bad guys take turns fighting the one good guy (deplorable tactics), so the hero gets to knock them off one at a time, without even getting winded. Then the conditions for Lanchester's law aren't fulfilled.

Another case in which the conditions aren't fulfilled occurs when the weapons available to one side are better than those available to the other. One heavyweight champion could easily clean up a dozen of the author's ilk, without having to draw a deep breath. Military folks like to call better weapons or skill "force multipliers."

But when the conditions for its applicability are in fact fulfilled, the square law has dramatic consequences. There was a period a while back in which two particular military fighter aircraft coexisted in the U.S. Air Force, the venerable F-4 and the newer and finer F-15. Fighter pilots (of course) preferred the new plane—it was hotter and more fun to fly. But alas, the old F-4, produced in vast quantities, cost just about $4 million per copy at that time, while the F-15 cost about $20 million. This author used to ask Air Force friends whether, in combat, they'd rather have one F-15 on their side or five F-4s, at the same cost. Almost always they favored one F-15, "because it's a better airplane." That's the answer you get without thinking. A factor of twenty-five advantage for the same price, obtained by squaring the numbers according to Lanchester's law, is not to be sneezed at. And in fact combat simulations (not widely publicized by the Air Force) amply confirmed the view that more is better. (In modern air-to-air combat, the missile you carry is far more consequential than the airplane that carries it.) But that fact pales before the lust to fly fine new aircraft, especially in peacetime.

The second important consequence of the square law is in tactics—that's why we've included this chapter in a book on decision making. It's just a shade less obvious mathematically. As the two sides in combat shoot at each other, there is what physicists would call a constant of the motion—a quantity that doesn't change as a result of the mutual clobbering. That constant is the *difference* between the *squares* of the number of units on each

side. For example, if a force of five units confronts a force of
three units under the proper conditions, the difference of the
squares is twenty-five minus nine, which is sixteen. The expected outcome of the combat will therefore be that the smaller
force will be wiped out, while the larger one will have four units
(the square root of sixteen) left. (Of course, real armies aren't
often so devoted to the cause that they will fight to annihila-
tion—this is a model.) Thus the larger force will have destroyed
an enemy force of three units with a loss of only one of its own. It
is that feature that has such important tactical implications,
where it is applicable.

Before getting to the details we might wonder if any of this
is true, or if it's so impossibly oversimplified as to be irrelevant
to real combat. The answer is both yes and no, to both questions.
There are certainly many cases in military history in which
badly outnumbered forces have managed to snatch victories,
sometimes because of superior weaponry, sometimes from superior positions, sometimes from better morale, sometimes from
being smarter, and sometimes from pure luck. No statistical observation will manifest itself all the time.

But, as we often say in the book, the name of the game is to
get the best *average* outcome from your immediate resources; on
that standard, Lanchester's law holds up remarkably well. One of
the most famous Pacific island battles in World War II was fought
to the last soldier (on one side), with no reinforcements, and it
was possible later to reconstruct the mutual attrition during the
course of the battle. It was astonishingly close to what might
have been predicted by using Lanchester's law. That's not really
surprising, since the underlying principles—the increase in firepower with numbers, and the dilution of the enemy firing effectiveness—are clearly applicable. All of this is well known to
military operations analysts, mostly civilians, but is resisted by
far too many high-ranking officers. It sounds sort of, well, mathematical, and that's not macho.

How could you in fact use this wisdom for decision making
in a tactical situation, supposing Lanchester's law to be exactly
right? Let's invent a simple case, in which you command a force
of fifteen units (let's call them men), confronting an enemy force
of seventeen equally competent men. You are outnumbered, and
have no special advantage in weaponry or position. In fact, since

the square of 15 is 225 and the square of 17 is 289, your opponent can wipe out your entire force, while 8 of his men survive (289 minus 225 gives 64, which is the square of 8). He will have suffered terrible losses, just over half his army, but you will be history. If it matters enough to him, it will be done.

But can you prevail anyway, in spite of (or because of) Lanchester's insight? You can if you can split the enemy ranks, and engage a part of his force with all of your own. Suppose that by some clever maneuver you are able to isolate 12 of his men, and can bring your entire army of 15 to bear on them, while his other 5 men are either asleep or trying to find the battle. Then, with Lanchester, 225 minus 144 is 81, and you can wipe out that separated force, keeping 9 of your original 15 men alive. Again, severe losses, 40 percent of your army, but victory. Now, of course, you have to deal with his other 5 men, but you have 9 men for the job, and have the advantage of numbers. By the time it's all over, you will have wiped out his superior force, and will have about half your troops left.

The upshot is that, though outnumbered, you have cleverly exploited the square law to split the enemy force in exactly the right way, and have been rewarded with victory. All military people are aware of the importance of breaking up enemy formations, and the idea goes under names like the principle of penetration, or the principle of concentration, but rarely as more than a qualitative concept.

There are many cases in military history in which an outnumbered force has prevailed, but not many in which it is possible to determine whether these principles have played a role. (Historically, an army doesn't surrender when it has been defeated, but when it *thinks* it has been defeated. It is sometimes possible to persuade it to perceive defeat while it is still the superior force.) The case that Lanchester cited as an example in his original work was the naval battle of Trafalgar, fought off the coast of Spain in 1805, in which Lord Nelson prevailed over a superior allied (French and Spanish) fleet. Lanchester claimed that Nelson instinctively knew where to cut the allied line optimally. Maybe so, maybe not—no one knows what went through Nelson's mind, especially since he was killed in the battle—but the principle is certainly right, and it wouldn't hurt modern Lord Nelsons to get a better grip on it.

Lanchester's law applies to combat between two forces shooting at each other; is there an equivalent for the case in which three combatants are battling each other? (Think, if you must, of the Muslims, the Croats, and the Serbs, in what used to be the contrived country of Yugoslavia.) Then there are two extreme possibilities. In one of them everyone shoots at all strangers (shoot first, sort later); in the other case two sides gang up on the third. The first is a soluble mathematical problem, somewhat too complicated for detailed treatment in this book, while the other is identical to the Lanchester problem, with the alliance considered a single force.

Let's do a specific case, with the numbers carefully chosen to lead to simple answers. Suppose the three opposing forces, called Alpha, Bravo, and Charlie, start with 45, 40, and 35 units (tanks, men, aircraft?), respectively, and then the shooting begins. Under Lanchester's rules everyone shoots at any stranger in sight, and they have equally good or bad aim. When the dust settles the smallest force will have been completely wiped out, while Alpha and Bravo will have remaining forces of 40 and 20 units, respectively. (Trust the author, it's not hard to do the calculation.) Not only will the minority force be history, but the second largest force, Bravo, will be badly depleted compared to Alpha. It will have lost half its original force of 40, while Alpha will have gone from 45 to 40. It will then be easy for Alpha to clean up Bravo, and emerge victorious with relatively small losses. A random shoot-out is a great arrangement for the largest force. Any shots that Bravo and Charlie have delivered to each other could only benefit Alpha.

But suppose the Bravo and Charlie commanders know all this, and make a deal to cooperate against Alpha (an alliance of convenience), reserving the settlement of their own differences for the future. Then the allied force starts with 75 units, vastly superior to those of Alpha, and can wipe him out with a loss of 15 of their 75. That's clearly better than self-immolation, which is the main reason alliances are so popular. (Of course, they don't always work out quite that well, because both members of the alliance are well aware of their own impending showdown, and are likely to hold back a bit. Allied support of the Soviets in World War II was less than enthusiastic, for this reason.)

There is a remaining question: the *relative* losses incurred by the Bravo and Charlie forces while in the business of crushing Alpha. That is, of course, what matters to each of them for the next round. Again, the mathematics is just a trifle too much, but the upshot is that each will lose 20 percent of his force, Bravo will be left with 32 of his original 40, and Charlie with 28 of his original 35, while in this case it is Alpha who is history. Bravo and Charlie will have suffered equivalent proportional losses in eliminating the common enemy. In the following slugfest Bravo will win, of course, but with grievous losses—he will end up with 15 or 16 of his original force of 45, and may well decide that it isn't worth it.

The moral that in a three-way contest it is always good for two to gang up on the third is a general rule that emerges directly from the theory of games with several players. Besides, we all know it from experience. (Even so, at this writing we are promoting a tripartite government of Croats, Muslims, and Serbs in Bosnia. It will not work.)

There is no reason to believe that the future military commanders now being trained (and even educated—training and education are two different concepts) at the three service academies are intellectually unable to learn about the principles of combat, even when it may involve some arithmetic. And the Secretary of Defense at the time of this writing, William Perry—by training a mathematician—knows all this very well. But at the next level it isn't deemed relevant.

The distinction between training and education is what makes the study of Lanchester's law important. Training involves conditioned response to known situations; education and intelligence pay off in unfamiliar cases. A friend of the author, a physicist, used to give speeches in which he said that you couldn't teach Newton's laws of motion to a dog. Someone once asked him if he'd ever seen a dog catch a Frisbee, and he had to change his speech. But he was right in the first place. A dog can be trained to catch a Frisbee—some dogs don't even appear to need the training—but it cannot be educated. Military officers can be trained easily enough, but education is needed when the situation turns unfamiliar. The combination produces the highest level of performance.

17

Fluctuations and Regression

The *Random House Unabridged Dictionary* (second edition), arguably the best of the current crop of big dictionaries, gives two meanings for the word *fluctuation,* but they contradict each other. One refers to wavelike motion, back and forth, the other to irregular motion, as in "the price of gold fluctuated wildly." Wavelike motion is fairly regular, as all sailors and surfers know, and in the case of some kinds of wave motion, can be so regular that you can set your clocks by it—our present standards for defining and measuring time are based on the most regular wave motions known to science, laser light waves. They are far more regular than the motion of the sun in the sky, the old way of defining time. Gold price fluctuations are an example of irregular change; otherwise we could all predict the price of gold and thereby become rich. (We'll go into all that in more detail when we talk about the stock market in the next chapter.)

In our case we are interested in still a third meaning of the word, more closely related to the second Random House meaning than to the first. It has to do with the relative unpredictability of random events.

Suppose we are throwing dice. We said in Chapter 3 that the probability of the dice coming up seven is one chance in six. So if we tossed honest dice a dozen times, we would expect to see a seven twice. Of course that won't happen every time we put together a dozen tosses—if we keep repeating the test, twelve tosses at a time, there will sometimes be no sevens at all, sometimes several, and it is even possible, though improbable, that *all* the tosses will come up seven. (The odds against that are over a

131

billion to one, but it *could* happen.) It is this kind of unpredictability of the outcome of a test governed by the laws of probability that we will call fluctuations. If we have nothing better to do than to keep repeating the test the outcome will indeed "fluctuate wildly," in the second Random House sense.

But how much will it actually fluctuate? Here there is a magic rule that tells you that for such a case, whatever the expected number of events (based on their probability) may be, the average fluctuation is just about the square root of that number. (That magic number is called the standard deviation. The rule doesn't apply in all cases, but in most.) So if we expect something to occur a hundred times, we shouldn't be surprised if it happens ten times more or less, perhaps ninety times; if we expect sixteen, twenty would be unsurprising. But remember that these statements about fluctuations are themselves probabilistic—in the dice-tossing case, all dozen tosses *could* come up seven, but we would be surprised. Very surprised indeed. In fact, the concept of surprise is central to old-fashioned statistics—if you have calculated that something has such a low probability that it would be surprising if it happened, and it happens anyway, then it is called "statistically significant." All the fancy term means is that you were pretty surprised. Not shocked into insensibility, just surprised. The word *improbable* is in the state of mind of the statistician; there is a kind of folklore among statisticians that a probability of one chance in twenty—called a *p*-value in the trade—makes an event sufficiently improbable (and therefore surprising) to deem it statistically significant. For the dice case, where we expected two sevens, more than four would be considered statistically significant by such statisticians.

The idea of surprise is psychological, and has nothing to do with mathematics or statistics. And what is surprising in one context may not be so surprising in another. Even the much used one-in-twenty standard for surprise among statisticians isn't so universal. Twenty-to-one shots often win horse races, just about one time in twenty, and not even statisticians are surprised. On the other hand, every decade or so we read a story in the newspapers about a bridge game in which each of the four players was dealt a perfect hand, all the cards of a single suit. Since the odds against that are worse than a billion billion billion to one, one would have every right to be surprised. This author, in fact, would bet heavily that it has never ever happened in a fair deal from an honestly shuffled deck.

But that is a digression. If there is an expected number of events, the fluctuations we would expect around that number usually simply follow the square-root rule. Although anything *can* happen, it usually won't.

But notice that, with the square-root rule, the fluctuations become larger as the expected number of events increases, but not as fast as the expected number itself. So the fluctuations become *relatively* smaller. If we expect a hundred occurrences, we expect fluctuations of around ten in the actual number observed. That is 10%. But if we expect ten thousand, the fluctuations will be around a hundred, only 1%. If you toss an honest coin once, you have no idea how it will land. But if you toss it ten thousand times, you ought to get around five thousand heads, give or take a hundred or so.

It seems to be very hard for gamblers and sports fans to reconcile themselves to the existence of fluctuations. Averages are reasonably well understood, but not the fluctuations around those averages. (We'll devote a chapter to sports later.) Consider an example.

In a typical professional basketball game, each team scores about a hundred points, and the shooting percentage runs in the neighborhood of 50 percent. (We're approximating all these numbers, just to keep it simple.) Since each basket is worth two points, each team takes about a hundred shots in a game, scoring about half the time. (Since the teams are allowed no more than twenty-four seconds to take a shot, and the game is forty-eight minutes long, that works out about right.) The standard deviation isn't quite equal to the square root for this high-probability-of-success situation—the formula is a hair more complicated—but turns out to be about five baskets, if the shots are independently random, instead of the seven you'd calculate by taking the square root of fifty baskets. Independent randomness simply means that each shot has roughly a 50-50 chance of going in, regardless of the success or failure of the other shots. With this model a team will score an average of a hundred points, with a standard deviation of about ten points. (We'll come back to streaks in the sports chapter.) So game after game a team's hundred points should vary up or down about ten points, occasionally more than that, and the winning margin (the difference between the two teams' scores) should be around fourteen points. (Never mind why.) All this is based on the simplest statistics, ignoring skill.

Any intrepid sports fan can, of course, check what the winning margin has really been through an entire season, but the average winning margin in the nineteen games of the conference finals and the championship series in 1993 (just before this was first written) turns out to have been less than nine points. That is somewhat less than we would expect by random fluctuations (assuming the teams are about evenly matched), but isn't far off for such a rough estimate. Certainly one factor that is likely to bring the two teams' scores closer together is psychological: the team that is trailing is likely to play harder, and the team that is leading to ease up a bit, or to play more conservatively, toward the end. What all this demonstrates is that much of the time the difference in the scores of the two (comparably able) teams is determined by random chance, rather than by any variation in skill from one day to the next.

But in the first quarter of the game, about a fourth of the points will be scored, and the fluctuations will be *relatively* greater. It will not be unusual for the ultimately losing team to be ahead at that point. When, later in the game, the laws of statistics begin to exert their ineluctable force, and perhaps the other team even takes the lead, the first team will be said to have "cooled off," though the real culprit may again be no more than statistical fluctuations. The tendency to run according to form in the long run, despite early fluctuations, is called regression to the mean, and seems to go against our instincts. Fluctuations are relatively larger in the beginning of anything, and play a less important role as time goes by. In the early part of a baseball season there is always some batter who is batting over .350, but he will be said to have cooled off later in the season. A good batter who is batting .200 in the early going is likely to improve later, as he regresses to his mean. It is not because he actually improves. At the beginning of the season some batters are ahead of their long-term norms, others behind. What's surprising about that? Of course, there will be long articles in the sports press about both, explaining it all.

That sort of consideration will apply to any game in which points are scored more or less at random, but not to a sport like football, where points are usually scored only after a long series of actions: first downs, two-yard gains, and the like, whose number tends to mute the statistical fluctuations. Remember the square-root rule.

It applies to other areas of life. Amos Tversky and Daniel Kahneman have pointed out that in the training of pilots, instructors often complain that if a pilot has performed badly, and is then severely criticized, he will improve. And if he has performed unusually well, and is praised, he will deteriorate. The instructor, of course, attributes this to some complex psychological influence, taking credit for the improvement, and blaming the pilot for the decline, but it is in fact mostly a normal regression to the mean, misread as a cause-effect relationship. Whenever you perform better than usual, you are not likely to keep it up—that's what the word *usual* means. That may be discouraging, but the converse is also true, and that is encouraging. And it is always bad for decision making to see causes where there are none. Regression toward the mean is an inevitable condition of life.

Finally, there is another, more technical, use for the term *regression*, which will be important later. The term is used to describe regression toward a *trend,* rather than toward a mean. Consider a new baby girl, weighing six pounds at birth. After a month she may weigh eight pounds, after another month of voracious eating, eleven pounds, then a month later, and after a cold, only twelve pounds, then fourteen, and so forth. If you look at these data, and plot them on a graph if you must, you quickly recognize that in these early months she is gaining an average of two pounds per month. Some months more, some months less, but the trend is clear. If you have gone to the trouble of drawing a graph, there is a pretty good straight line that goes through the collection of points, though some points are above the line and some below. Still, the line is what would be called a decent fit, and the gain of two pounds per month is a pretty good estimate. That is what statisticians would call a regression, an approximation to a trend line—in this case a linear regression. A good deal of statistical practice is devoted to isolating trends from masses of data, and there are dozens of computer programs on the market that will do the job for you. Feed them the data, and they will regurgitate the regression. (Nowadays, people who have no understanding whatever of what they are doing can turn out impressive charts and displays. It's the information revolution—an abundance of data, beautifully organized, but less information.)

Such analysis is big business, and is the most commonly used method for making "predictions" about the future. Once you have drawn the regression line, you can extend it into the future, and call it a prediction. It is not based on any wisdom or understanding of the forces at work, but in cases in which past trends do continue into the future, it can do reasonably well. Trend analysis through regression is the lifeblood of companies and countries, with the unspoken assumption that whatever mysterious forces were causing something to increase in the past are still around, and will cause it to increase in the immediate future. It works for the baby's weight gain, for the federal deficit, and for the world's population, inter alia. Big bucks are spent in analyzing trends in the stock market, through more or less sophisticated regression analysis, because the ability to predict tomorrow's stock prices is money in the bank. If anyone has discovered the key to consistent success there, it is still well hidden. As in all such matters there are fluctuations in the degree of success different investment advisors have in different years, and last year's hero may well (because of regression to the mean) turn out to be tomorrow's bum. We'll devote the next chapter to this apparently fascinating subject. Despite the enormous stakes, most investors (and their advisors) know very little about the statistics of the stock market. And it is appalling what garbage many of them believe (and sell).

So what have we learned? There are unavoidable fluctuations in all statistical processes, you shouldn't mistake short-term results for long-term indicators, regression toward the mean is inevitable and should not be read as indicative of changes of skill, and real trends can often be (cautiously) identified through regression analysis. All of these insights contribute to rational decision making.

18

Investing: The Stock Market

Of course, there isn't just one "stock market." There is a bucket-ful of market forms that go by similar names, all involving some form of ostensibly open bidding procedures for fungible products, like a Middle Eastern bazaar. Most of this chapter will apply to nearly all of them, but the underlying assumption of everything we say will be that they are run honestly. If some of them seem to run on the ragged edge of honesty—inevitable, given the temptation—so be it. This chapter should have no influence on corporate tycoons or high political officials, who have access to profitable information not available to the rest of us. Use of such information is sometimes blatantly illegal, sometimes not so blatantly, and sometimes even legal, but that is in any case not relevant to the art and science of decision making. The thought calls to mind the famous admonition of a minister to his flock; he urged them to always tread the straight and narrow line between good and evil. He probably didn't appreciate what he was saying, but that may be the best way to beat the market, while still avoiding outright crime.

The question for us here is whether decision theory is of any help in finding optimal investment strategies. The countryside has been flooded with computer resources over the last decade or so, and that has fed a wild proliferation of programs for the analysis of stocks. It is clear that the idea has caught on, rightly or wrongly, that there is profit to be found in computerized analysis of the stock market. Of course, the mob feature that goes with sale of the very same programs and algorithms many times over to otherwise independent investors can undermine the diversity needed to maintain a fair and stable marketplace. When everyone has the same computer program, good or bad, and that program tells everyone to buy or sell stocks at the same time, rightly or wrongly, the result can be chaotic. It happens from time to time, and people seem to forget that the computer program they are using was written by people who are often no wiser than they themselves may be, and who are simply in the business of selling such products. But once the lore is embedded in a computer program, it takes on a life of its own. (Every author knows this—when you see your book or article in printed form it looks far more authoritative than it ever did as a manuscript.)

The classic example of mob psychology in the financial markets was the great tulip craze in Europe in the early seventeenth century. (The delightful book *Extraordinary Popular Delusions and the Madness of Crowds,* by Charles Mackay, is a fine source for this and similar sobering events.) Investment in tulips reached a level at which people were paying the equivalent of a year's income for a single bulb, confident that, whatever they paid, they could sell it for more in a month or so. It was a madness that ultimately collapsed of its own weight, just like any kiting or chain-letter scheme. The word *tulipomania* is now in nearly all good dictionaries. And with modern mass communication we are more vulnerable than ever to financial panics, either way.

The basic premise of all the exchanges is that the price of a stock (or whatever is traded on that particular exchange) is fairly determined, through open competitive bidding on the part of potential buyers, and open competitive offers on the part of potential sellers. (Just as for tulips, even an agreed price can be a bad guide to real value, but it's necessary to agree on a price before a transaction can take place.) Since the stocks for sale are, like dollar bills, completely interchangeable (one common share of XYZ Corporation has the same value as any other common share—that's what the word *fungible* means), there is no reason for a buyer not to buy at the lowest price available, and no reason for the seller not to take the highest bid. There are nearly always *some* buyer and *some* seller who can be brought together by simple haggling, and the deal is cut, millions of times a day. The markets have elaborate but imperfect mechanisms to assure investors (and also to assure the Securities and Exchange Commission) that this openness is in fact in place, and the brokers collect commissions from both buyers and sellers for providing the exchange service. We'll just have to suppose that all this works, though of course private deals abound, and many are entirely legal. Scandals show up as regularly as robins and worms in springtime. The incentive is certainly there.

Competition on the part of both buyers and sellers is essential to the stability of the arrangement, just as it is in other parts of a market economy. If there are few buyers to bid against one another, the buyers can force the eager sellers to lower their asking prices. If, on the other hand, there is a wide range of buyers and sellers, there will always be *some* buyer willing to pay a price acceptable to *some* seller, and the market is thereby maintained. So in a truly competitive market, in which there is no collusion among buyers or sellers, equilibrium is found at a set of prices mutually acceptable to at least *some* members of each side, according to their individual estimates of the value to them of the stock in question. Monopoly on either side is fatal to a market based on competitive bidding, but it can be prevented only by law and its enforcement. Collusion pays well, and is mighty attractive to the players who think they can get away with it. That's why the Securities and Exchange Commission was created in 1934, in the heart of the Great Depression.

But in a fair market, what goes into the various estimates of the value of a share of stock? It is ultimately a piece of paper, not particularly good to eat, and presumably (though not always) too valuable to burn in your fireplace. With the march of computerization it will undoubtedly soon be nothing but a set of electronic blips in magnetic or optical storage on a computer somewhere, with even less nutritional or fuel value. It represents part ownership of something with the potential to earn current and future income, the latter increasingly uncertain as the potential investor seeks to look further and further into the future (with, of course, suitable discounting of value). And the investor has to compare the projected utility of stock ownership against other available investment instruments, like bonds, bank accounts, real estate, fast food franchises, or burglar tools.

Some future expectations don't depend much on the specific stock in question, but on the overall health and prospects of the national, or world, economy. Such considerations can drive the whole population of stocks higher or lower in desirability, therefore value, and therefore price, regardless of the particular merits of individual stocks. So the value of a stock depends on a bundle of specific and nonspecific factors, and the art and science of determining the relation of price to value is what investing is all about. Stocks of stable and reliable companies tend to sell at prices between five and twenty times their current annual earnings, depending on special circumstances, while speculative investments—stocks of companies that offer the prospect of a killing in the future—may sell at a high price even while the companies they represent are losing money hand over fist.

So expectation of future profit plays an important—traditional textbooks would say pivotal—role in setting stock prices, and the analysis of such expectations fuels a giant industry of soothsayers and analysts. There are so-called fundamental analysts, who concern themselves with the earnings potential of individual companies with either promising products or good management or an exceptional work force, or whatever else bodes well for a company's future. There are others who barely know the name of a single company (a slight exaggeration, call it poetic license), but specialize in predicting the broad trends of the economy, the prospects for particular industries, and such matters—things that tend to drive the prices of large groups of stocks. Literally millions of investors follow these recommendations, more or less loyally. (There are also the astrologers, the spiritualists, the tarot card readers, and other less obvious phonies, but we'll ignore them here.)

Because bidding is competitive in a fair market, the agreed price between a diverse group of buyers and an equally diverse group of sellers, both having the same facts available, represents, in a sense to be expanded below, a "market" price for the stock at hand. It should represent the averaged wisdom of the community of buyers and sellers about the value of that stock, and should represent the value to which an individual would come if he had all that information handy, and weighed it evenhandedly in his analysis. (In the strict sense of the word it is not an average; it is what the most eager buyer will pay the most eager seller, at any given time.) This is what the experts call an "efficient market," and an individual can only "beat the market" by knowing more than the other participants in the efficient market know, or by analyzing it better or faster than they do. The simple version of the theory behind the efficient-market picture is that there are so many people out there doing these analyses that any fact that may affect the value of a particular stock is instantly widely known, is instantly assimilated into the collective consciousness, and instantly makes evident its effect on the price of the stock. Someone will act on the information—quite a few people are well paid to do exactly that. And indeed some tests do show that news and rumors travel mighty fast in this environment. So the efficient-market picture is that it is futile to hope to beat the market if you have available to you only the information and the analytical tools available to your competitors—everyone else. Or you can be smarter than they are, or work harder, with the information everyone has available. When individual investors thrive year after year (like the legendary and now retired Peter Lynch of Fidelity Magellan), it is in large part because they spend more time than most in reading and understanding the affairs of individual companies, and therefore do in fact know more than the competition. There is no reason why diligence and skill shouldn't count, even in investing. Of course, in any given year someone without either diligence or skill will do well, but, as we've often emphasized, that can be the luck of the draw—a fluctuation, in the sense of the last chapter. Guru for a year is more the norm than the exception in the investment business.

Another presumed path to riches is analysis of overall stock market statistics, in the hope of identifying trends. That would be in the spirit of the last chapter, and such an analyst could avoid going through the agony and hard work of selecting individual stocks. Here the picture is a bit murkier and more complex, but we'll give it a shot. For this kind of thing we must work with averages, rather than specific stocks, though we'll come back to something in between, in the end.

First and foremost, what makes the market averages change from day to day? Sometimes the market reacts to news, good or bad, that may have an effect on the future prospects for investment. When the Federal Reserve Board changes its interest rates, the stock market jumps, though it's not always clear in which direction. (That depends on whether the change was anticipated or unanticipated. And if anticipated, whether the guesses were high or low. And whether investors think that what actually happened was in fact anticipated. When people buy or sell stocks or bonds in anticipation of an interest rate change, they may be right or wrong, but are always contributing to the efficiency of the market.) Similarly, news of war, peace, political events, and so forth, all affect the market averages, and it is profitable to be able to predict those effects better than the competition. The everyday fluctuations in the averages are the composite of lots of little factors and a few big ones, affecting different stocks and different investors, and adding up to something like the random walk that we attributed to the drunk in Chapter 5.

But how random are the fluctuations in fact? On a typical day on the New York Stock Exchange (the day this is being written) about a thousand stocks scored a gain, another thousand a loss, and about seven hundred were unchanged. If the changes were really random in the traditional sense, and the stocks behaved independently, we could apply the square-root rule, and expect the number of gainers to differ from the number of losers by about the square root of a thousand, or about thirty. That turns out to be about what it was (actually forty today, which is just as reasonable), so by that crude test, the individual stocks are just wallowing around like our drunk near the cliff. In that picture the composite averages are behaving like the center of a mob of a few thousand drunks.

That kind of analysis has been done in considerably more sophisticated detail over long periods of time, and the consensus (though not unanimous—nothing is in this business) is that the daily variations in the stock averages do indeed resemble a random walk, with little discernible pattern. (That's consistent with the efficient-market picture, which suggests that if there were any kind of exploitable regularity, it would have been found, and would have exerted enough influence on the price structure to compensate for itself.) If you accept the picture, it is as hopeless to use the averages for pattern recognition as it is to figure out which way a drunken mob intends to go—and this despite the large sums spent by investors, and collected by prognosticators, for just this kind of analysis. But the evidence isn't crystal clear, and hope springs eternal, so gurus and other kinds of gambling entrepreneurs thrive and prosper. (The famous Peter Lynch, mentioned above, recently gave an interview in which he was so quick to denounce the random-walk model that he convinced this author that he doesn't quite understand it. You don't have to know everything to be successful in using what you do know.)

Suppose we take the next step, and ask just how much of the daily variation in the averages over a longer period can be accounted for by the cumulative effects of random walking. (Remember that a random walker does drift away from his starting point, over time.) This can be analyzed the same way, by using the square-root law and its more sophisticated siblings. Again the evidence is convincing, but not crystal clear, that the daily and weekly and monthly variations in the averages are mostly due to random and uncoordinated fluctuations in the individual stocks that make up the market, added up like the drift of the drunken walker. It is a fallacy of human perception to see patterns that aren't there, and to see order where there is none. Beauty and order are in the eye of the beholder. (In the Aristophanes play *The Clouds,* Socrates tries to convince the character Strepsiades that the chorus, which has just come on stage, is really made up of clouds. Strepsiades protests that they look like people, and says that he has never seen a cloud with a nose. But Socrates asks if he has ever seen clouds that looked like leopards or lions. Well, yes. . . . Soon Strepsiades is convinced.) But again the evidence supporting the random-walk model isn't crystal clear—it's adequate to meet a reasonable standard of judgment, but inadequate to convince doubters who take it too literally. Those who doubt may be wrong, but they need not be unreasonable. (That reference is to educated doubters of the random-walk model, not to pattern-matching soothsayers. The latter, because they are not accountable, are free to be unreasonable.)

One can take still another step in understanding nonrandom outcomes of random walks. Just as our drunk in Chapter 5 came closer and closer to the edge because his world was tilted in that direction (in the roulette example, the odds slightly favored the house), there is a difference between up and down in stock prices—they can go through the top, but not the bottom. The analogy that comes to mind is a comment made by a flight instructor fifty years ago, when this author first learned to fly. It is depressing to be in a small airplane in a downdraft so strong that it is impossible for the underpowered training plane to maintain its altitude, and it can be more than depressing if this happens close to the ground. It can easily happen in the lee of a hill, and one simply finds oneself losing altitude, approaching the hard ground, and powerless (in both senses of the word) to reverse the trend. The instructor's reassuring comment was that there is no record ever of a downdraft blowing an airplane completely into the ground. Of course she was right; even the air can't go through the ground, so there is a natural bottom to downdrafts, which always turn as they approach ground level. (This has nothing to do with wind shear near the ground, which is a genuine hazard for all aircraft, large and small, and is often confused with a downdraft in the popular press.)

Stock prices also can't go through the bottom—no one will pay you to take a stock off his hands—so there is a natural barrier that creates a difference between up and down, just like the cliff edge for the drunk. Except that, in this case, like the ground for the airplane, the bias is *up,* not down. In the end, that means that price changes are more likely to be up than down. Technically, for readers in the know (everyone else must skip the rest of this sentence), it means that the distribution of stock price changes is asymmetric, and suggests that it may be better approximated by a skewed distribution of the type known as lognormal, tilted up, than by a normal distribution. If this actually happens, the changes will be more relative than absolute—not equal chances of going up or down ten points, but similar chances of going up or down 10 percent. If a stock happens to have gone up 10 percent, the next 10 percent will be larger than if it had gone down, and that adds up to gains in the long run. So a random walk of this kind is similar to the random walk our drunken friend had, but tilted toward higher averages. The cliff edge has become a cliff wall. There is considerable evidence that this kind of biased random walk accounts for some share of the long-term upward trend in the stock market averages. But by no means all of it—at this writing the twenty-year bull market is aging and gasping for breath, but still breathing. (In fact, there have been extensive statistical studies of the long-range behavior of the stock averages, and experts differ on the extent to which it differs, if at all, from a truly lognormal distribution. The most important discrepancy is that large changes in the averages, both up and down, do seem to occur somewhat more frequently than a lognormal distribution would suggest. For those who love long words, that means that the distribution of changes in the averages exhibits leptokurtosis. That subject, and its many fanciful interpretations, is beyond our mathematical ambitions here.)

Up to this point we have been speaking as if each stock price goes its own way, oblivious of the behavior of others; that assumption was at the heart of our use of the square-root law above. Of course that isn't entirely true, and we alluded earlier to the more global forces that affect stock prices: rumors, facts, government action or inaction, economic forecasts, wars, stories in the *Wall Street Journal*, television pseudo-experts, and so forth. These tend to affect many different stocks in much the same way, and it is just wrong to pretend otherwise. And stocks vary among themselves; some are bound to be more sensitive to market forces than others. How can that be measured?

Well, not surprisingly, there is another cottage industry making that kind of analysis, correlating the changes in individual stock prices with those of the stock market averages. It is generally done through regression analysis, of just the sort we mentioned in the last chapter—plotting on a graph (or suitable computer surrogate) the price changes in a given stock against the price changes in the market as a whole. The ratio of these two, as measured by fitting a straight line to the graphical data, is called the beta (the second Greek letter, β) for the stock. If the beta is two, that means that a 1 percent change in the averages will lead, again on the average, to a 2 percent change in the price of that particular stock. (Of course, since the averages are nothing more than the averages of a large group of stocks, the average beta for all stocks is bound to be reasonably close to one. It doesn't have to be exactly equal to one, partly because the standard used to calculate beta, normally the Standard and Poor's 500 index, doesn't represent all stocks. Even for the index stocks, if they are not properly weighted the beta will not be exactly equal to one—high-priced stocks tend to fluctuate proportionately less than low-priced stocks, which affects the average beta.) Brokers and others can provide tables of the value of beta for nearly all stocks, and even for mutual funds, some of which have more speculative investment policies (and therefore portfolios) than others. Beta is sometimes called the volatility.

This is important to investors for an essential reason: the value of beta is considered by many to be an important measure of the risk associated with a particular stock. The rationale is simply that an investor is supposed to be very reluctant to lose everything, and investment in a stock that can go down 50 percent when the overall market only goes down 10 percent is a bad deal (though we'll see in a moment why it may not be so bad). Therefore, to the extent that the value of beta is *perceived* to be a measure of risk (and perception is as important as fact to many investors, and therefore to the price of a stock), it should be expected that stocks of higher beta (risk) will command a lower price than might be justified by their actual value. But lower cost means greater expected gain, so investors are generally perceived to trade risk for possible gain in buying speculative (high-beta) stocks. In the language of decision making, the subject of this book, the utility of a stock is reduced by its risk, so the price must be comparably reduced to produce a decision to buy. Speculative portfolios carry great risk along with their potential for great gain.

There is an additional fact we need. Just as a particular stock tends to follow the more-or-less random walk of the market averages, to the extent measured by its beta, individual stocks are also subject to random influences of their own. Directors resign or are appointed, products are announced, quarterly reports are issued, rumors fly, accidents occur, strikes are threatened—all these may affect a particular stock without much effect on the market averages. So individual stocks follow a random walk of their own, in addition to their beta-related share of the market walk. It is as if our imaginary drunk, representing the market, is holding the long leash of his equally drunken dog, representing a particular stock, who wanders around randomly from the drunk's own random position. The amount to which this happens depends on the particular stock (or dog), and there is no general rule, but the stock-specific randomness of many stocks is just about as large as the overall market average randomness. Again, there are analysts who can supply this kind of information, for what it is worth (or perhaps for more than it is worth—we'll see how to reduce its effect through diversification).

The asymmetry between gains and losses mentioned above plays an even greater role than we have admitted. If, as in the example of Chapter 4, there were an even-money chance of losing half your stake or doubling it, you should expect to gain in the transaction. (If you make two ten-dollar investments, lose half of one but double the other, you'll be five dollars ahead.) Similarly if stocks change their prices proportionally to their starting price, a wide-ranging stock is more likely to end up ahead. The advantage to be gained by the asymmetry increases with the volatility (beta) of the stock in question, so people seeking to make a killing should be speculators. Except that there is a certain probability that they will go broke in the effort—just as in our earlier gambling examples.

So, starting at the turn of the century with the Ph.D. thesis of a young French mathematician named Louis Bachelier, but actually taking root in the last couple of decades, a marvelous way to have your cake and eat it has been developed. (The thing that astonishes this author, a physicist, is that it took so long for the investment community to catch on to this one. It is completely routine among physicists to use this technique to reduce what we call noise in an experiment. The idea was put on a solid mathematical foundation in 1809 by the great German mathematician Carl Friedrich Gauss. That the investment community did eventually catch on is clear from the amount of gainful employment the large investment houses now provide for physicists and mathematicians.) All that is necessary to achieve a win-win situation is to be speculative, but diversified.

What this has come to mean is that you should fill your investment portfolio with speculative stocks, but so many of them, and so different from one another, that although there is a risk that any few of them may go down dramatically, there is a far lower probability that they will *all* go down at once. The basic idea is simplicity itself: if you own ten stocks in roughly equal dollar amounts, and just one of them goes up by a factor of ten, it hardly matters what happens to the others. Even at their worst they can't go through the ground. Of course this simple idea has complex implications that can be couched in more mathematical terms, but that is its essential core.

There are many stock-advisory services that maintain what they call "model portfolios"; they keep records, though they may or may not actually invest their own money in their own portfolios. (Give no credence whatever to those who don't. They have no incentive to make good decisions unless they themselves have something at stake.) These model portfolios will usually include an "aggressive" portfolio, often consisting of fifteen or twenty stocks, and some of these portfolios do quite well. If you look at the detailed makeup of one of those you'll probably find that it is made up of a batch of losers, mixed in with one or two remarkable winners. The few winners, perhaps only one, more than make up for the rest. So the fundamental idea of diversification (to reduce overall risk), combined with speculative purchases (to increase the chance of hitting a real winner) is catching on, and is used by more and more investment advisors for the management of large individual stock portfolios.

But stop, you may say. Doesn't the efficient-market model tell you that if everyone learns about this, the prices of the chosen stocks will necessarily rise, and ultimately wipe out the advantage now held by the practitioners of this relatively sophisticated art? The answer is that of course it will happen, and it is already happening. Because the incentives are so great, no advantage in analysis or method can stay effective for long in an efficient marketplace. It is only because some methods require a level of statistical or mathematical sophistication that is not held by the vast majority of investors or investment advisors, that there is even a temporary advantage. But while it is there, it is there. And the reduction in the inherent risk of the speculative stocks appears only when they are held in a diversified portfolio, which is not always the case. Besides, the efficiency of the market is imperfect, if only because the sophistication of most investors is limited. (Anyone who actually reads this chapter will be far more sophisticated than the average investor.)

Finally, back to the random-walk picture of stock fluctuations—how good is it? There are statistical tests that can be applied to any collection of numbers, to determine whether they can be treated as if they were as likely to be random as to have been generated by some mysterious hidden force. (The dream of finding such a magic force drives many investors.) Taking the last ten years as an example, the broad market averages have increased about 8 percent per year, or about a seventh of a percent per week. By contrast, the average variations (fluctuations, standard deviation) around that rise have been about ten times as much, over the same period. So, while people marvel constantly about the great bull market of the last twenty years, in fact the "random" variations have been much larger than the steady rise, when measured by the weekly changes. (We'll stick with weekly

closing prices for trivial reasons—in the span of human existence daily is too short, and yearly is too long.)

One of the simplest tests for randomness that can be applied
to a time sequence (and stock prices form a time sequence) consists of looking for runs up and down. A run up is a sequence of
prices in which each closing average is larger than it was the
week before. If a sequence is truly random, runs of only one will
occur about half the time (on a given day or week, stocks are as
likely to go up as down), runs of two about a third of the time,
runs of three about an eighth of the time, and so forth (it isn't obvious, so don't worry about it). The actual data for a couple of
market averages for the last ten years (as tested by the author)
show a small deviation from this rule, with runs up tending to
be a bit longer than runs down (as befits a generally rising market), but neither average differs greatly from the picture of large
random fluctuations in stock prices, on top of a small drift
upward. It's in that environment that market-prediction gurus
must function. Among scientists and engineers, that is known as
finding the signal in the background noise—like listening for
a pin dropping during a rock concert. It cannot be done by consulting your navel. It's not clear that it can be done at all. Mind
you, this is all about averages—some individual stocks do soar,
and some collapse. If you know the secrets before everyone else,
you can profit.

What has all this to do with decision making? It simply
means that the problem is complex, and that any effort to apply
solid decision-making methods to optimizing gains in the
stock market has therefore to be sophisticated, and has to deal
with these confounding statistical features. The get-rich-quick
schemes, pattern watching, searches for three ups and a down,
and so forth, are not going to be of much help. Anyone can see a
pattern in the record of stock prices, just as anyone can see a pattern in cumulus clouds. On the other hand, the evidence seems
to suggest that the functioning of the stock market is not exactly
a random process, nor is the market entirely efficient, so investment, like all other activities mentioned in this book, is likely to
reward the diligent and the informed, at the expense of the lazy
and the uninformed. In ignorance there may be bliss, but not
earned wealth.

19

Gambling

Gambling has an ambiguous status in our society. It is widely accepted, widely practiced, and just as widely denounced. Our ambivalence toward it mirrors our public attitude toward the pleasures of sex—both suffer from the legendary Puritan ethic, which has long outlasted the Puritans. There is in fact no explicit or implicit derogatory mention of gambling in either the Old or the New Testaments, the religious books most familiar to this author (who is not a student of comparative religion, and therefore cannot comment about other religious teachings). Games of chance show up in a number of places in these books, usually as a means of obtaining divine guidance—Joshua cast lots to determine the distribution of land, for example. In those ancient times no one knew what we now know about probability, so it must have seemed natural to assume that what seemed to be unpredictable events were in fact determined by higher will, for its own mysterious reasons. What better way is there to communicate with these higher forces than to invite them to influence something we can see or hold? (This will come up again in the chapter on law.) That view has a lot of persistence—the number of people who still believe in the fortune-telling power of such things as tarot cards defies common sense. It was not until the work of Geronimo Cardano, a mere five hundred years ago, that we know of any serious effort to analyze games of chance in terms of probabilities.

In the simplest games, the only decision-making problems are whether or not to play, and at what stakes. Slot machines (one-armed bandits now undergoing an electronic mutation to zero-armedness—evolution at work) are simplest. There is nothing for the gambler to do but feed them money, in the hope that they will be kind enough to give something back. The player usually doesn't even know the odds (though he can be sure they are unfavorable), so the decision to play or not to play is made in almost complete ignorance. Despite this, millions of people do play, in the almost certain expectation of loss. At this writing, such machines, once confined to the few states that permit legal gambling, are proliferating through Indian reservations in those states in which they would otherwise be illegal, and are finding homes on gambling boats in states with nearby water. The unspoken rule seems to be to keep them out of sight, but within reach, and arrange for a minimal cut of the take to go to some worthy cause. The payoff ratios (the amount you get back, on the average, for the money you put in) vary with location, and are generally withheld from the public, despite the push toward truth in merchandising that we see elsewhere in our late-twentieth-century society. A random selection of slot-machine payoffs recently seen by the author ranged from about 90 percent to 97 percent, depending on location and level of the slot. (Dime slots usually have a lower payoff than dollar slots, presumably to cover the overhead.) Imagine a label that says: ON THE AVERAGE THIS MACHINE WILL ONLY KEEP 5 PERCENT OF THE MONEY YOU FEED IT. Truth in labeling, where are you when we need you?

All games of this sort have the same simple logic, like the roulette example in Chapter 5. You will almost certainly lose in the long run, but have a chance of coming out ahead in any given session, if you can find the strength of character to limit your exposure. If the entertainment value is more important to you than the cost, just recognize what you are paying for the fun. (We mentioned in Chapter 5 that if you watch people playing these machines, it doesn't usually *look* as if they're having fun, but for humans intense concentration can sometimes look like misery.) Still, people do make other impulse purchases of unneeded items, and it is healthier to squander your resources on gambling than on cigarettes. For games like slot machines, all that is necessary is to know the odds, and then to make an informed decision about how much you are willing to lose—on the average.

There are two small embellishments to the roulette example, which apply to coin tossing and other games in which the odds are even, or close to even, and the stakes are even, or slightly worse than even. In the roulette case, we came to the casino with $1,000, and wanted to leave with $2,000—it turned out that the best strategy was to go for broke on the first bet, in which case there was nearly an even chance of winning. But suppose your needs are even greater than that, and you have to turn your $1,000 into $10,000—what are your chances, and what is the best way to optimize them? Well, it's the same general rule: play hard, and throw caution to the winds, for a while. You'll probably lose everything, but you have a small chance. But suppose, on the other hand, that you have staked your entire bankroll, starting with the original $1,000, and have luckily won your first three bets (with a probability at, or just below, one in eight). You now have $8,000 in your pocket—should you now put the full $8,000 on the next bet? That would be wrong, because you would be risking everything for the chance of going way over target, to $16,000. No, the best strategy at that point would be to bet only $2,000 on the next toss. If you win, you quit with your needed $10,000, but if you lose you still have $6,000 to work with, and can bet $4,000 on the next play. So the best strategy for this kind of game is to bet the farm if that doesn't take you over target, and otherwise bet just enough to get you there. It can be proven mathematically that there is no better way to play such a game. (That was a carefully worded sentence. There are other ways that are just as good, but none *better*. One that is just as good, for example, is to pretend at the beginning that your objective is $5,000—for this example—and use the previous strategy in the hope of getting there. If—at a chance of one in five, as we'll soon see—you do make it to $5,000, then bet the farm. That gives the same chance of winning as the straightforward strategy, if the odds are nearly even.)

But that leaves one final question: if you use that optimal strategy, and hope to parlay your original $1,000 into a stake of $10,000, what are your real chances of making it? It turns out that you can't do better than a chance in ten of multiplying your bankroll by a factor of ten, even with the very best strategy. That's a general rule for fair (or almost fair) games: The probability of achieving your objective before going broke is exactly the inverse of the amount by which you want to increase your fortune. Or somewhat less if the game is somewhat less than fair. Not entirely obvious, but true. And if the game is ever-so-slightly less than fair, and you play cautiously, you can count on losing.

The general rule that your chance of doubling your bankroll is nearly one in two in a fair game, and tripling it is one in three, and so forth, actually has deep roots. In a probabilistic world (the one we happen to live in), the expected value of your fortune is the product of a probability and a sum—there is no long-run difference, always on the average, between having ten dollars and having a coupon that entitles you to an even-money shot at twenty. Or a one-in-ten shot at a hundred. Psychologically they are vastly different, but not mathematically—we say that the expected value is the same. In the long run, you are no better and no worse off.

That principle is worth keeping in mind, because it is completely general. It also means, of course, that if you go into a casino with the objective of becoming immensely wealthy, you have an infinitesimal chance, even with the best strategy. Fantasies of striking it rich may be fun, but they are still fantasies.

Finally, one more embellishment for this kind of game, and we'll use real roulette as the example. Up to now we have only used red and black betting in roulette, but roulette is much more complicated than that. A roulette wheel traditionally has thirty-six colored holes, numbered from one to thirty-six, and one or more holes labeled zero, or double-zero, or even more imaginative markings. A typical American wheel has two such holes, while the traditional European wheel has only one. Half the numbered holes are red and half black. We've been speaking in terms of the American wheel, and will continue to do so.

There are many ways to bet on roulette. The player is paid even money if he bets on red or black, or if he bets on even or odd. He is paid at thirty-five-to-one odds if he selects a particular number, two-to-one if he bets on a particular dozen of the thirty-six numbers, and so forth. The odds on all of these would be exactly fair if there were only the thirty-six numbered and colored holes on the wheel, but the casino owner rakes in a bundle when the zeros appear. And that happens, on the average, one spin in nineteen on an American wheel—about half as often on European wheels. For all of these bets, just as for red and black, the optimal strategy if you absolutely need to gamble to meet a need, is to bet as aggressively as possible, forgoing the entertainment for the chance of gain, and to quit when (if you are lucky) you have met your objective. You simply must have settled on your objective in advance, or you are doomed. And in all such strategies, the best you can do is to come close to a probability of winning that is the inverse of the amount by which you want to multiply your fortune. So at the roulette table you don't have to play a sequence of even-money bets to gamble for a big bundle; you can fill in with the two-to-one options, or others, as long as you minimize your exposure to the long-term odds. They always favor the house.

Now one admonition to the compulsive gambler. Even if you wallow in self-control, and follow the optimal strategy *for a night,* you cannot do it night after night, and still preserve your chance to come out ahead. In other words, you can't resolve that you will surely quit when you have doubled your wealth, play earnestly and optimally toward that objective, and then come back the next night to try the same stunt. Our description of the optimal strategy is good for one try only—if you are a compulsive gambler, you will lose as surely in the long run as if you had played cautiously, no matter how slightly the odds are tilted against you. So if you really need to gamble night after night, you might as well bet cautiously, enjoy the entertainment, and call your inevitable losses the price of admission.

For slightly more complicated games, the odds may not be as easy to calculate—we gave an example in Chapter 3 for a poker hand—but a serious player can find them out. (For poker, there are plenty of books containing the odds, and it is, of course, a competitive game—good players have an edge. Craps is a simple exercise, and every reader should by now be able to calculate that you have a chance in three of making a point of four or ten.)

Sometimes the odds are deceptive or unknown or ignored. We mentioned the lotteries in Chapter 5, where the odds against winning the grand prize are either not understood or are deemed irrelevant by those who read in the newspapers about others who have won. The it-could-have-been-me fantasy takes over, and indeed there can be some rationale for taking the chance, in terms of the utility of money.

But only if it's close. This author recently read a news item about a casino that housed a simulated video-poker game—it was proudly proclaimed that the payoff for a royal flush was five hundred to one. That may seem high, but the actual odds against a royal flush in an honest simulation (calculated exactly the same way we did four of a kind in Chapter 3) are a lot closer to a million to one for a pat hand (to be exact, one chance in 649,740), and worse than a chance in twenty thousand in draw poker. Odds of five hundred to one are a shameless scam on the uninformed, and no reader of this book should fall for that.

In fact, if there is one single lesson about gambling decisions that transcends all the subtle ones about the proper strategy for a given objective, it is that no strategy can be effective, even at limiting your losses, if you don't know the odds. (The only exception to that rule is that you can't lose if you don't gamble, whether or not you know the odds.) Even if your mathematical skill doesn't include figuring out the odds of a big eight at craps, or whether it makes sense to draw to three of a kind in draw poker, there are books that will tell you more than you really want to know. No one should be embarrassed at having to look things up in a book—it's a great habit to develop. If they won't let you bring a book into the casino, memorization of numbers is good exercise for the brain. Most of our brains need exercise. Of course, casinos are on the lookout for people who appear to be mathematicians—one friend of the author has been thrown out of dozens.

We've been using red and black at roulette as our example of a simple game, bearing in mind the fact that, though a typical casino will pay you even money, your chance of winning is only 47.37%. So the house (with a 52.63% chance of winning) has more than a 4% advantage over you, guaranteeing its long-run triumph.

But are there more generous games at a typical American casino, assuming that you are willing to pay for your entertainment, but want to limit your costs? You bet there are. This is a book about decision making, not gambling, but the decision to go to a casino, followed by a decision of what game to play, fall into the general pattern of knowing your objectives and knowing your probabilities, so the choice of game is a fair subject.

First, to repeat an old point, casino operators are not in business as a public service, so there is no way you can win in the long run. You can only hope to slow the rate of loss for the same amount of entertainment. In that vein, red and black in roulette is one of the worst bets in a typical American casino. Consider craps, for example, one of the most venerable of all games, in which a pair of dice is thrown, and the simple rules are these: On the first toss two, three, or twelve lose, while seven or eleven win. If none of those five possibilities shows up on the first toss, then the number that does come up is called the point, and subsequent tosses end when either the point comes up again, or a seven comes first. The point wins, and a seven loses. Simple enough—the methods we described earlier lead to the conclusion that the odds are slightly against the shooter, who will win 49.293% of the time. Compare that with the 47.37% of red and black at roulette, and one would have to be either ignorant or eager to lose money to choose roulette over craps, *if* he got even money in both cases.

But wait, those are the real odds—the casino doesn't pay off in terms of the real odds. They count on winning, so they generally adjust the odds accordingly. Casinos differ, but the usual pattern is, in fact, to pay even money on a pass (that's what it is called) at craps. The casinos operate on a razor-thin edge, compared to roulette. At craps you can also bet against the shooter, but the casino typically makes the odds the same by not paying if the shooter shows a twelve (boxcars), which should happen one time in thirty-six. (That makes it very slightly better to bet against the shooter, but the difference is negligible. The casinos have access to people who know how to calculate odds—it's their business.) So gamble at casinos if you must, but go to the craps table, if the odds are as discussed here. If not, go to a different casino.

There is another betting option in craps, worth knowing if you are really determined to pay for your entertainment at the craps table. Most casinos will allow you to augment your bet after a point has been established, to the tune of the original bet or even twice as much, *and will pay honest odds on the additional bet.* Since there is no house edge on the additional stake, it pays to make the original bet (on which the house has its advantage) as small as possible, and the "free-odds" bet as large as the rules allow. In other words, as much as possible of the money you have decided to risk should be devoted to the additional free-odds bet. That way the house will still collect your money in the end, but will take longer to do it. If you do this consistently, and the casino will permit a free-odds bet of twice the original, you can improve your probable return from 98.586% to 99.394%, which is beginning to look almost respectable. But remember, it is still less than 100%, and you will still lose in the long run!

Of course, at both roulette and craps there are far more ways to bet, each with its own preferred strategy, but it would use too much space to deal with them here—the lesson is simply to always know your odds, and never to bet blind.

And games are different. There are actually systems for blackjack that give you a slight statistical edge over the house, but casinos are alert for players who appear to know too much. Our mathematician friend who gets thrown out of casinos likes to play blackjack.

Up to now we've dealt with noncompetitive games—you against the house and the immutable laws of probability—for which the best strategy is calculable. But there are interesting competitive games used for gambling, like horse racing. Horse racing, you might say, is competitive only for the horses, but you'd be dead wrong. The post-time odds in a pari-mutuel system are determined entirely by the betting choices of the addicts, the entire take (less, of course, the cut for the management, which is between 15 and 20 percent) is paid out to the winners, and there are nearly always winners. A person who bets at the racetrack is not betting on horses, but on people. Just as in the stock market, the key to success is to be better than the competition, not better than nature. This can be accomplished either by skillfully picking winners, or by having inferior competition. Or, of course, by cheating, if you can get away with it.

In fact, betting on racehorses has many of the characteristics of the stock market, in that much (but not all) of the relevant information is available to anyone with the energy and initiative to track it down. And there is certainly plenty of incentive to do so. To see this, consider a purely imaginary situation in which it is discovered by diligent research that people have a visceral bias against horses with long unpronounceable names—they just sound slow, dragging all those funny letters around. The name has nothing to do with speed, but if people shied away from betting on such horses, regardless of their speed, the payoff would be a shade higher than it ought to be when they do win a race. So people who know that foible would have an edge in the long run, just by betting on horses with strange names like Xybblwzddm. But there are so many thousands of people reading the form sheets, and going to the races, and even making their living through the racing business, that the word would soon get around, more people would jump on the bandwagon, and the odds on Xybblwzddm would go down. In the end, in a fair and open marketplace, they would settle around the real odds of success for such a horse, and this particular way to exploit human frailty would stop being profitable. That's how an efficient marketplace works. (In all honesty, this author doesn't know if names like Xybblwzddm are acceptable to the racing authorities. He doesn't bet on horses—oops, people.)

But that is all theory so far—is it really true? Well, the way to find out is to look up a few thousand races, and see whether the odds at post time really settle down to a fair estimate of the probability a horse will win a race (or place or show, which we've ignored here). Take all the five-to-one shots (horses paying twelve dollars for a two-dollar bet) for a year or so, and see if they win about a sixth of the time. It's been done by many people, and the consensus is that it's very close—the post-time odds are an amazingly good estimate of the actual probability of winning, and there is little money to be made at racetracks by trying to outguess the betting crowd. But they aren't perfect—there is a small tendency for people to put more money on long shots than they should, and a shade too little on favorites. It's easy to think of psychological reasons for this—the fantasy of a big win, the disdain for betting two dollars to win one dollar on an odds-on favorite, and such other manifestations of the utility of money. But it's close enough for the track's cut to wipe out any rational chance to make money from those idiosyncrasies, in the long run. The most recent study of this subject (by folks with statistical credentials) known to the author was by Brown, D'Amato, and Gertner, published in the statistical magazine *Chance,* in the summer of 1994.

Many "systems" for winning at the races have been invented and published, and some even have solid statistical underpinnings. One popular system *assumes* the efficient marketplace, and therefore takes the betting odds just before post time to correctly reflect the probability that each horse may win the race. That means that the pari-mutuel odds are fair (apart from the cut that goes to the track), so there would be no gain in betting to win at those odds. However, there are ways to use the winning probabilities to infer the chance that each horse may come in second or third (place or show, in the jargon of the trade), and the betting odds in the place or show pools may or may not be right. It's a harder calculation, with a shakier foundation, and most bettors simply can't do it. There can then be an inefficiency in the marketplace for place and show bets, and an informed person with a modern hand calculator can often make last-minute bets that are advantageous. This particular system was published in the early 1980s, and made sense at that time, but now so many bettors use it that the former inefficiency probably no longer exists. That is, after all, how an efficient marketplace works. Remember that an efficient marketplace does not require that every investor or bettor be wise, only enough of them to matter.

All of this presumes that the games we are discussing are fairly played. This author admits to being a bit cynical on that point, given the stakes. Where there are high stakes there is a strong incentive to find a way around the rules, and where there are strong incentives there are those who respond to the challenge. They don't all get caught. Of course that can't be proven, either way.

We will resist the temptation to analyze other games of chance—the pattern is clear. Know the odds, be clear about whether you are betting against people or things, and be clear about your objectives. Above all, don't expect to win in the long run if the odds are fair or worse. Unless, of course, you are a good poker player, lucky enough to have (at least for a while) friends who aren't.

20

Sports— Mainly Baseball

Back in 1964 (second edition in 1966) a splendid book called *Percentage Baseball,* by Earnshaw Cook, was published. Legions of operations analysts had been trained in World War II to apply systematic probabilistic techniques to strategic and tactical problems, and it was natural for them to look now to sports applications. After all, many of them had played these very sports as children, and the compulsion to apply new knowledge to familiar problems is irresistible.

The resulting work has had almost no effect on the day-to-day activities of the practitioners and coaches of the various sports. It is as if there were a world of long-haired eggheads who crank out scholarly papers, and another world of tobacco chewers who actually play the games, more or less as their mommies and daddies did. There have been other books since Cook's, but not many, and similar analyses of other sports, but not many. It's odd, since there are thick tomes of statistics about baseball, there are thousands of major-league games played each year there isn't a strike (just over a thousand games a year in those days, and more now), and the mind-numbing details of each game are dutifully reported in the press and preserved for posterity. One would think that since professional baseball players and managers are presumably in the game to win, they would be eager to seize any tool available (legal, of course) that might help. For example, they could find out from the data whether, on the average, it pays to intentionally walk a batter with a man on second base and no one out, or whether a bunt is called for if the base runner is on first base, and there is one out. Cook and his successors have analyzed a mass of data about many of these traditional tactics, and more often than not the research has shown that the reputations of these maneuvers are not justified by the facts.

Computers are widely used in professional sports, but mostly for data accumulation and storage during and immediately after games, to search for weaknesses that are being exploited by the opponents, and to search for opponent weaknesses that can be exploited. It is the sorting and collection capability of computers that is being used in such cases, not the capability for the kind of sophisticated analysis that challenges the ancient strategic precepts of a game. Opportunities exist as much in the sports world as in the business world, where computer simulations are widely used, and have had a major impact.

So in the spirit of an efficient marketplace, one would expect the word of this capability to get around, and professional managers to adjust their behavior to the ineluctable laws of probability. After all, a strategem at baseball is not too different from a gamble at a casino or a plunge in the stock market—you should play with the odds most of the time, but gamble boldly on the few occasions when time has run out, and there is a great deal at stake. In a long baseball season there is plenty of time for the laws of probability to establish their ascendency, so there is no rational excuse for fighting them. You would therefore think that every major-league manager would have the probabilities memorized, as does every professional poker player, but, alas, it ain't so. Cook's book is long out of print, and only a handful of books found by the author in the research for this book even mention the subject. And George Will's otherwise marvelous book about baseball, *Men at Work,* doesn't even have the word *probability* in the index. It does, however, often mention luck. Baseball *could* be a percentage game, but isn't. Given the *average* player's salary (at this writing well over a million dollars a year), it can't be for lack of education. Can it?

Let's start with an example that we used in an earlier book: the chance of a perfect game. That's simple, and easy to work out, so it makes the point better than most options.

A perfect game is a game in which the pitcher retires all twenty-seven batters who face him—no runs, no hits, no errors, no walks, just pitching perfection (or batting ineptitude—take your pick). The reason the probability is easy to work out is that the process is easy to visualize—the pitcher has to retire the first batter he faces, then the next, then the next . . . If the probability of retiring each batter is 0.7 (just about right, according to data that have been collected over the years), all you have to do to find the probability of a perfect game is to multiply 0.7 by itself twenty-seven times. That's easy on today's hand calculators, and the answer turns out to be about one chance in fifteen thousand. All you've really assumed is that each batter presents a new case to the pitcher, with a chance of 0.7 of success in putting him out. There are now over four thousand chances per year at a perfect game (each pitcher gets a chance, so there are two chances per game), though there used to be fewer, so you'd expect a perfect game every three or four years, less frequently in the days when there were fewer teams and shorter seasons. At this writing there have been eight such games in the so-called modern era, starting with Don Larsen's in 1956 (in the World Series!), which is not at all inconsistent with the expectations, given the square-root rule of Chapter 17. So the basic assumption we made, that each batter has more or less the same chance of being retired, works out just fine.

This is a general feature of all such sports. Though all managers and professionals speak wisely of streaks, and of batting slumps, and of hot hands in basketball, the evidence is routinely consistent with the view that there are no such things, and that observers are notoriously bad in judging whether something is random or has a systematic pattern. We went through this in Chapter 8, when we discussed Shannon's guessing machine, and again in our discussion of the stock market in Chapter 18. Whatever it is in people's brains, they like to see order when there may not be any. That's actually a deep and important subject, which deserves better than a chapter on sports in a book on decision making.

But if it is really true that sporting events are governed by an underlying probability (determined by skill, height, weight, training, and other matters) on which there are simply random fluctuations that can be mistaken for patterns, then the decision-making rules we've been talking about in this book should be widely applied. Cook's book in 1964/1966 was an effort to make that possible, and it had little or no effect on the actual practitioners of the game, professional or amateur. It is fashionable in modern America to sneer at mathematics, nowhere more so than in sports. Of course, some managers absorb the lessons of mathematics without formally knowing any, and it's possible to go part way with that approach, but there is no real substitute for knowing what you are doing, in decision making or in anything else. (See John Paulos's provocative little book *Innumeracy* for the flavor of the problem.)

In order to simply multiply probabilities, as we have been doing, we have to be sure they are not correlated (correlation means that if one thing happens, it influences the probability of another); otherwise it would be wrong to assume that the events happen more or less independently. There have been many studies, on various sports, that show lack of correlation to be more the rule than the exception. The reason is clear in baseball, which is largely a series of encounters between a batter and a pitcher, with or without prior outs, and with or without men on base, but repetitive throughout the game. Why shouldn't there be relevant statistics? Hockey, soccer, and basketball are sequences of forays down the ice or the field or the court, each independent of the previous one, so why shouldn't statistics accumulate? A baseball season is a sequence of encounters among the same teams, over and over again during most of a year, as repetitive as one can imagine. Of course, every game is different, but from a loftier view they are also all alike. One can actually examine whether, *on the average,* it pays to bunt. (It doesn't.)

On top of the war-generated blossoming of interest in and respect for operations analysis (the best-known achievement was helping to find German submarines in World War II), there has come the dawn of the real computer age. There are surprisingly realistic games available for all sports, but again most specifically baseball, that have internal workings that faithfully reflect the observed statistics of the games, and in some cases even of specific teams and players. So it is now not only possible to bring formidable analytic tools to the analysis of sporting events, one can even test candidate ideas about novel strategies, rejecting the ones that don't work. Just as flight simulators are immensely useful in training pilots, and battle simulations in training soldiers and generals (not all of whom are soldiers), one would expect game simulations to help train baseball managers. Of course, that is a pipe dream. But one can at least collect the data and the analyses, hoping for a more sophisticated day to appear.

To illustrate the potential, we can look at the outcomes of the best-of-seven World Series, and see if 4–0 series victories (sweeps) occur as often as, and no more than, they should. If each game is independent of the ones that have gone before, and if the teams (each the winner of its league championship) are pretty evenly matched, then the distribution of wins ought to be pretty close to what you would get by flipping a coin. (Of course, the great New York Yankee teams of the distant past are an exception to the "evenly matched" assumption.) That's a pretty simple picture, and ought to provide useful information. Cook did this for 1903–61, and it worked out pretty well. We've collected the last fifty years of experience (at this writing in 1994— the year the series was canceled for a players' strike) to do the same test.

With these assumptions, the chance of a 4–0 series should be one in eight; any team can win the first game, but then the same team must win the next three, at even money each time. One can easily do this kind of calculation (or just go through all the options systematically, as we did for poker in Chapter 3), and the results for the probabilities and expectations are as follows.

outcome	4–0	4–1	4–2	4–3
probability	0.125	0.250	0.312	0.312
expected	6.25	12.5	15.6	15.6
observed	7	8	11	24

Remember that all this rests on two important assumptions: that the two teams are evenly matched, and that the games are independent events, with the teams coming in with clean slates for each one. As we emphasized in Chapter 17, we can expect statistical fluctuations around the expected values, by amounts not much more than the square root of the expected numbers. So to expect about six 4–0 sweeps and to observe seven is not at all surprising. The square root of 6.25 is 2.5, so a difference of two or three would be reasonable, and the closeness of the observation to the expectation is better than we had any reason to anticipate.

But you don't have to look much further to become a wee bit nervous. We're on the ragged edge of acceptability for 4–1 and 4–2, both coming in well below their expected frequency, but way out of line for a series that goes the limit to 4–3. Thirty percent of all series should go the limit, and we have nearly half—twenty-four out of fifty. That's twice as far away as our rough square-root limit. (There's a fancier statistical test we can use, called the chi-squared test—chi is the Greek letter χ—and that tells us that this kind of discrepancy should happen by chance only one time in twenty.) So something here is just a bit surprising. Of course it is *possible* that this is the result of pure chance, and is simply a statistical fluctuation, but the approximately twenty-to-one odds against it suggest that we should think a bit harder.

Well, we've made only two assumptions, so now is the time to question them. The assumption that the teams are evenly matched doesn't help; if that weren't true it would work in the wrong direction. If one team were really much better than the other (as in the glory days of the Yankees), it would make a one-sided series more probable, and therefore reduce the number that go all the way to the limit. We have the opposite problem: too many go to 4–3.

All that's left to question is the assumption that the games are independent, without which there could be some correlation that pushes toward a long series. Player incentive doesn't work, since it was decided long ago to pay the players (at least over the counter) only for the first four games, for just this reason. It could be management strategy—a manager who is ahead by 3–2 may decide to save his best pitcher for a possible seventh game, thereby making it more likely that he loses the sixth, extending the series to seven. That would be a questionable strategy from the point of view of probability (compare gambling strategies in the last chapter), but wouldn't be surprising. Finally, there is the incentive of the owners and television networks, who stand to make an extra bundle if the series lasts longer. People have whispered about that kind of incentive for many years, but there is no hard evidence that there is any tampering. Still, even with the best of intentions, and with people reeking of honesty and integrity, it is hard to ignore the plain fact that a longer series pays almost everyone better. It's even more entertaining for the public. We are not in any way suggesting any misbehavior on anyone's part, and it may well be that the discrepancy is purely and simply a matter of statistical fluctuation.

But let's follow the track just a bit further. Any series that goes all the way to 4–3 must have been tied at 3–3 just before that. And any series that is tied at 3–3 must have been at 3–2 just before that. But if a series score is 3–2, and the teams are evenly matched, it is equally likely that the leading team or the trailing team will win the sixth game. Therefore 4–2 outcomes and 4–3 outcomes should be equally probable, and should occur in approximately equal numbers. In fact, as our table shows, the series went all the way to 4–3 twenty-four times, and ended at 4–2 only eleven times. So in the thirty-five World Series we're looking at, the ones that went through the 3–2 phase at some point, some leading team or manager did *something* that increased the chance of losing the sixth game. (Or the other team, faced with ultimate defeat, played unusually well. We won't take that option seriously, since these are all professional teams, in the World Series, and there is no reason to believe they don't always play as well as they can.)

If the strategy that led to the disproportionate chance of a leading team losing the sixth game were as simple as holding back your best pitcher, one wonders whether managers would do it if they really believed that it gave them more than a two-to-one chance of losing today's game, followed by a presumed even chance of losing the series in the seventh game. It might not matter even then, because decision making in baseball is intuitive, not calculated.

Another possible explanation is that the tendency to go all the way is built into the scheduling of the games, because a seven-game series must involve four played at one stadium and three at the other. Since there is at least some level of home-team advantage, one would expect the scheduling alone to tend to draw the series out. The unfortunate fact for this theory is that, though the home-team advantage is clear enough in basketball, it is only a small effect in baseball, and not nearly enough to explain the number of 4–3 series. Of the last fifty World Series outcomes, the team holding the home-field edge (four games scheduled at home, though it's only gone all the way about half the time) has won exactly twenty-five times. If there is an advantage at all, it isn't much. (It is not entirely clear why it is so much larger in basketball than in other sports. It may be that basketball is especially dependent on stamina toward the end, and the home team is better rested. Or it may be the influence of the crowd on either the players or the officials, despite the professionalism of everyone involved. We are all free to speculate.)

There remains the possibility that this aberration in World Series outcomes is simply a fluctuation, due to the laws of chance and nothing more. (It didn't show up in Cook's analysis of the World Series for 1903–61.) One can calculate the probability that it could happen by chance, and the answer is a chance in fifty, about the same as being dealt three of a kind in poker. Such things happen, but not as often as we think, so it *could* be chance.

Baseball, the most statistics-afflicted sport there is, is fair game for amateur decision-making buffs to second-guess, and it is truly amazing (at least to this author) how many of the hallowed traditions don't stand up to reasonable scrutiny.

For example, there is a batch of managerial maneuvers designed to optimize the situation on the bases for the offensive or defensive team—to increase or reduce the probability that the team at bat will score. For the offensive team, one of the familiar tactics is a sacrifice bunt, when there is a man on first and no one out. The idea is that a man on second is in "scoring position," while it normally takes an extra-base hit or multiple hits to score a man from first. But the raw statistics show that it is generally *bad* to give away an out—you have only three to use up in each inning, and they are precious commodities. Specifically, an advance of one base for a base runner, at the expense of an unnecessary out, is usually a bad trade—the probability of scoring goes down. Those are the facts, contrary to most managers' experience and instincts. Pit a fact against an instinct, and an instinct has a better-than-even chance of prevailing.

Similarly for the practice of intentionally walking a strong batter, when there is a man on second and either no outs or one out. This is supposed to enhance the probability of a double play, or a force out at third, both relatively rare events—though managers tend to selectively remember the times they worked.

Here the defensive team is putting a man, and a potential run for the opposition, on base, with no price whatever. Again, the data show that this will normally result in more runs for the offense, not fewer.

There is a popular saying among engineers, "Don't confuse me with facts, I know what I'm doing." At what point do you go with the facts, despite what your intuition and experience tell you? Cook's book opens with a purported quotation from Francis Bacon, to wit:

> In the year of our Lord 1432, there arose a grievous quarrel among the brethren of a monastery over the number of teeth in the mouth of a horse. For thirteen days the disputation raged without ceasing. All the ancient books and chronicles were fetched out, and wonderful and ponderous erudition, such as was never before heard of in this region, was made manifest. At the beginning of the fourteenth day, a youthful friar of goodly bearing asked his learned superiors for permission to add a word.
>
> Straightway, to the wonder of the disputants whose deep wisdom he sore vexed, he beseeched them to unbend in a manner coarse and unheard of, and to look in the mouth of a horse to find an answer to their questionings. At this their dignity being greatly hurt, they waxed exceeding wroth; and joining in a mighty uproar, they fell upon him, hip and thigh, and cast him out forthwith. For, said they, surely Satan hath tempted this bold neophyte to declare unholy and unheard of ways of finding truth contrary to all the teachings of the fathers!

Just to further emphasize that it always pays to check the facts, it has turned out to be impossible to verify that that wonderful and enlightening story did in fact originate with Bacon; efforts to find it in his collected works have so far failed. But it is a good story, very similar to one (also probably concocted) told about Aristotle, who is said to have declined to look into his wife's mouth when a dispute arose about whether men and women have the same number of teeth. Same story, same lesson, and same level of authority. Presumably, in this age of "infomercials" and "docudramas," we shouldn't be offended when people take liberties with the truth. But we are—it degrades the public decision process. So the story above is a fine story, with a solid lesson, but we have come to doubt Cook's attribution to Bacon.

Back to baseball. Recent statistical studies of the game, always by statisticians and not baseball people, consistently confirm the view that the events of any particular game as it unfolds, and the outcomes of any series of games, are relatively disconnected, and that any appearance of patterns is a figment of active imaginations on the part of the viewers of the game. We keep emphasizing people's propensity to see patterns that aren't there—it is a human failing that is deadly in the decision-making business. It is in distinguishing real patterns from fictitious ones that experts are distinguished from cultists, and professionals from amateurs, whatever the subject at hand. In sports, far too many professionals are amateurs in understanding the statistics of their own sports.

Every competitive sport that involves teams alternately scoring points, with the maximum score determining the winner, can be regarded as a stochastic process. A stochastic process is not as mysterious as the fancy term suggests; it simply means that the game goes through a sequence of states or conditions, that at each one there is a certain probability of proceeding to each of the next possible states, and so forth. Thus, in basketball, the teams run down the court, the offensive team may or may not score, the ball may or may not be stolen, either team may commit a foul, and so forth. For each of these there is a probability, and the game goes back and forth this way. Most statistically sophisticated sports analysts have assumed that the various sports are well described by a particularly simple form of stochastic process, in which the outcome probabilities for the current state don't depend on how you got there. Thus, in football, when a team gets the ball it hardly matters whether they got it through a punt, an interception, a fumble, a kickoff, or whatever. They have the ball somewhere, the offensive team is on the field, and that's all that matters. Obviously that is somewhat oversimplified, but the analysis shows it to be a pretty good picture. It is best in basketball and hockey, and not quite so good in baseball. But good enough.

We've spent most of this chapter on baseball—does this general pattern of looking down on real data also pervade these other sports? Well, to the extent that there is more analysis done and published in the statistical and management journals than is read, let alone understood or believed, by athletic professionals, yes. Still, the investment community also used to be indifferent to statistical work on its underpinnings, and it is only in recent years that there has been an explosion of interest in professional statistical analysis of stock portfolios. (There has always been pattern watching, the astrology of investing.) Two things brought this about, the explosive growth in the availability of fine computers, and the discovery that one can in fact make more money by doing the job well. One would expect that since both of these factors are also present in professional sports, they will one day leave their mark, but that day remains in the future.

21

The Lady or the Tiger?

In many decision-making problems the player (decision maker) has to choose one of several options, given just a wee bit of partial information, or sometimes none at all. The prototype of all such quandaries may be the famous 1884 short story "The Lady or the Tiger?" by Frank R. Stockton. (For those who don't remember, the king in that story is in the habit of punishing miscreants by sending them into an arena with two identical doors at one end. Behind those two doors are a ferocious tiger and a beautiful maiden, respectively, and the transgressor must pick one. The fate of those who pick the tiger is clear and immediate; those who pick the maiden must marry her on the spot, whether or not either of them has a preference. It is obviously assumed in the story that the errant soul is male, and that the maiden is to be viewed as a prize—not at all politically correct these days, on either count. One day a handsome but otherwise undistinguished courtier is caught in an affair of the heart with the king's daughter, and is duly sentenced to the traditional punishment in the arena. Before the event the king's daughter manages to learn which door will hide which surprise, and agonizes at length whether to send her lover to his death, or permanently to another woman. There are no other choices. Finally, at the arena on the fateful day, he catches her eye, as she knew he would, and she signals him to the door on the right. He opens it. End of story.) Such stories have developed into full-fledged decision-making challenges, and have become sufficiently popular to deserve a chapter of their very own.

Start with a different form of the Prisoners' Dilemma, in which a prisoner has heard through a usually reliable source in the prison grapevine that two of the three prisoners currently held are to be released the very next day. He is delighted, and the jailer—a person he has learned through long experience to trust—verifies that it is indeed true. The jailer even knows who they are, but isn't volunteering the information.

Of course the prisoner (call him Tom, and the other prisoners Dick and Harry) realizes that his chance of being released is two out of three, a probability of ⅔, but he is understandably eager to know more, and he wonders if there is anything he can do to find out. The obvious move is to ask the jailer straight out, but he is afraid that a direct approach might somehow jeopardize his chances. So he considers a roundabout run at the problem. He reasons that, since either Dick or Harry will be released, regardless of his own fate, it can't do any harm to ask the jailer for the name of some other prisoner who will be released.

But then he stops to think. Suppose the jailer says that Harry will be released. That will use up one of the two releases, leaving the other one to either him or to Dick. That would make it even money for him, since he has no advantage over Dick, and he will have lowered his chances from 0.667 to 0.500 just by asking. So he doesn't ask. Does that make any sense?

The distinguished statistician Frederick Mosteller included this puzzle in his popular book *Fifty Challenging Problems in Probability with Solutions,* and reported there that "Of all the problems people write me about, this one brings in the most letters." Mosteller concluded that, no, he hasn't lowered his chances by asking the question, and they remain two out of three, even after the question has been asked and answered. We won't repeat his argument at this stage, but will come back to it after we deal with the most recent flap over a closely related familiar problem, a flap generated by Marilyn vos Savant, a columnist for *Parade* magazine. We will see that the logical dilemma is the same.

This one can be called the switching problem, and the uproar occurred when a reader of vos Savant's column asked her for the answer—reputedly she has the highest IQ yet measured, and is indisputably extremely intelligent. (This author has sampled some of the intelligence tests she has breezed through, and can assure any skeptical reader that her performance is mighty impressive. People who claim there is no such thing as native intelligence are nuts.) The question to vos Savant was posed more or less as follows.

You are appearing on a game show (there once was a similar show on television) in which the host shows you three doors, numbered one, two, and three, telling you (truthfully) that there are goats behind two of the doors, but a fine car behind the other. You will get what is behind the one you pick, and we need to take it for granted that you'd rather have a car than a goat. (There is no accounting for tastes, so that's an unstated assumption. In this kind of thing you have to watch out for unstated assumptions.) You select door number one, but the rules of the game are that after you have made your selection, but before your selected door is opened, the host will open another of the doors, and give you a chance to make a switch. So he opens door number three, revealing a goat, and now asks you if you'd like to change your mind, and switch your choice to door number two. This is your decision problem: to switch or not to switch. Think upon it.

Vos Savant reasoned more or less as follows: When you selected door number one, you had one chance in three of picking the one with the car, which means that there are two chances in three that the car is behind one of the other two doors. Now the cooperative host has shown you that it is surely *not* behind door number three, and the chances for door number one haven't changed, so there are two chances out of three that the car is behind door number two. In effect, the probability that was reserved for door number three has been transferred to door number two. So of course you should switch. (Mosteller's conclusion was the same, but with a rather more detailed line of reasoning.)

Just as Mosteller reported a flood of mail about his answer to the prisoner puzzle, vos Savant says she received thousands of letters about the game show problem. *Parade* is very widely circulated, and the vast majority of letter writers thought she was wrong. The most common answer supplied by the correspondents was that it was now even money between doors one and two, often using Tom's argument above—that you've narrowed it down to two options, and don't know which, so it's equivalent to a coin flip. Interestingly, vos Savant provided another informative datum: of the letters from the general public, 90 percent thought she was wrong, while letters from universities were only stacked 60 percent against her. In the ensuing ruckus, a number of Ph.D. statisticians weighed in with their views and their passions, more on the side of even money than otherwise. Vos Savant was clearly taken aback by the ardor elicited by the problem, and by the force of the opposition, but stuck to her guns. (It's hard to resist an editorial comment—good for her!)

(Though it's out of sequence, note the relevance of this dispute to the place of majority rule in dealing with the complex matters that arise in government and with the legal issues we'll discuss in the next chapter. Do we make technical decisions by popular vote in a democracy? If not, how do we protect the public? The answer 50-50 would clearly have carried the day here, if the matter had been put to a vote. And a screwball value of pi would have carried the day in the Indiana Legislature, had a passing mathematician not caught the legislators *in flagrante delicto.*)

Professional statisticians have fought, and still fight, over the answer to the game show question, despite its disarming simplicity. Anyone can understand it, and can even put himself in that position. It is even easy to simulate: use three cards facedown to serve as the "doors," one ace and two deuces to represent the car and the goats, and play the game a few dozen times. You'll find out soon enough that switching is beneficial, as claimed by vos Savant. So what's the fuss, and why do experts disagree, and what is wrong with the argument that makes it even money after the goat is found behind door number three? Or is there some unstated assumption being made by all the players, even when the game is being simulated with cards?

The marvelous fact (and this is what makes the puzzle so educational) is that there is *nothing* wrong with either argument, though they come to opposite conclusions, and therein hangs a tale. (There is an old joke about King Solomon, in which two neighbors argue before him, and after each neighbor's pitch the king says, "You're right." A passing lawyer hears this, and says to the king, "But they can't both be right," to which the king replies, "You're right, too.")

There is missing information in the puzzle as stated, but all the players (including vos Savant) have made unconscious assumptions about this missing information, mostly not even noticing that it is missing. This is not meant as a dig at vos Savant—she clearly believes that her assumption about the missing information is so obvious that the information really shouldn't be considered missing. So, however, do those who make the opposite assumption believe that *theirs* is entirely natural and obvious. So natural and obvious do these opposing views seem to the two schools that neither notices consciously that an assumption has been made.

Enough of speaking in riddles—what's going on here? Should the player switch? Well, the sound way to approach any problem in decision making is to make clear what the various options are, even before assigning probabilities to them. In this case, before the host gets into the act, there appear to be three options, the car behind doors one, two, or three, and there is certainly no preference specified in the terms of the game. So it is reasonable to assume an honest game, and therefore to assume that the starting probabilities are just as stated by everyone, ⅓ for each of the three doors. So far so good.

Now the player—you—picks door number one, and there is again no magic there. You know nothing, and the chances that you are right are as stated, one in three.

But now the fun begins, because the host has opened door number three, and *no one has asked why he chose that one.* There are several possibilities here, and the information conveyed to you by his choice depends on what you know in advance about his own internal rules, so far undisclosed. He could, for example, have promised his mother that he will *always* open door number three if the contestant selects number one, whatever is behind it. It would then just be fortuitous that this time there was a goat—had it been the car, the game would have ended there, and you would have lost. If that is his reasoning, then the fact that there was no car behind the door is indeed additional information to you, and the location of the car has indeed been narrowed down to door number one or door number two, with no known preference. The host hasn't given you any reason to switch to number two, nor any reason not to. The vast majority of vos Savant's correspondents, who believed that the odds were now even, were unknowingly making that assumption about the host's strategy. In most cases they probably didn't even recognize that they were making it, but felt they were right.

They doubtless wondered how such an intelligent person as Marilyn vos Savant could have made such a silly mistake.

But suppose the host had made no such promise to his mother, and is governed by another set of rules. He might feel that he should never open the door with the car behind it, because that would end the game prematurely, and destroy the suspense surrounding the decision of the player. That would cost audience interest, and he is in the entertainment business, so this wouldn't be an unreasonable policy on his part. So if the host's strategy is to never open a door with a car, *and* you've picked right in the first place, he can open either door two or door three, as he pleases. *But,* if you picked wrong in the first place, and the car is really behind either door two or door three, he will open the other. So he will always be able to open a goat door, and gives you no information whatever when he does so.

Wherever the car is, he hasn't affected the chance that it is behind door number one, your original choice. But if the car is not behind it he has told you which of the other two has the prize. So two-thirds of the time—when you weren't right in picking door number one in the first place—he has told you which of the other two to pick. If this is his strategy, vos Savant was right—switch while you have the chance, and glory at your good fortune. It doesn't mean you're sure of winning if you switch (there's a chance in three that you were right in the first place), but it doubles your chance.

This is a case in which both of two fiercely contending sides can be right, depending on the internal rules governing the host. If he opens at random (or according to his promise to his mother), and the car is not behind the door he opens, then the odds have truly switched to even money. If he has long decided never to open the car door at this stage of the game, then he has given you a peek behind door number three, and you ought to use that information by switching.

Now the really hard and interesting question: what if everything happened just as described, but you actually knew nothing of the host's strategy, and were ruled out of order when you asked? Then you are back to the state of affairs of the genie paradox of Chapter 9, in which there is vital information (in that case the genie's intentions and bank account) that is simply not available to you. If you do your thinking properly, you will recognize that the right strategy depends vitally on the host's state of mind, and he's not about to tell you that. Then you will simply have to make a guess, just as was necessary with the genie, and the decision about whether to switch will be the better, the more accurate your psychological analysis of the host. Isn't that the way it is in life? What is quite clear is that it will never hurt to switch, because even if the host had made the promise to his mother, the odds are even, and you would lose nothing. Vos Savant was right.

Finally we can come full circle, back to "The Lady or the Tiger?" The star-crossed lover in the arena is signaled by the king's daughter to open the door on the right, and he does so. Had the story been written recently, instead of over a hundred years ago, decision theory would have been invented. Then, undoubtedly, the unlucky man would have thought through the conflicts that must have occupied the princess's mind, made his best judgment about what she probably decided was in *her* best interests, and then proceeded in such a way as to optimize his chances for a happy future. Stockton gave us only the first move. And hardly anyone has read Stockton's sequel to "The Lady or the Tiger?" This would be a good time to do so.

22

Law and Juries

Thomas Paine, the great pamphleteer of the American Revolution, began his best-known pamphlet, *Common Sense* (February 1776), by saying that society is made necessary by our wants, and government by our wickedness. Think about it. Laws are an expression of the goals of government, not of society—they tell us how wickedness is defined by the government, how much of it will be tolerated by the government, and what punishment will be inflicted by the government on those who are caught exceeding the acceptable bounds. It is when we try to define wickedness, measure the bounds of wickedness, and mete out the appropriate punishment to transgressors, that law turns into decision making.

Those seeking advice about legal questions will have no trouble finding a lawyer—there are nearly a million of them in the United States, nearly twice as many as there are doctors, and more than in the rest of the world put together. And we have less than 5 percent of the population of the earth. Legal services cost Americans well over $100 billion per year, nearly five hundred dollars a year for each and every one of us, and the average income of lawyers tops that of any other profession. To boot, there are twice as many lawyers per capita in this author's home state of California as there are in the rest of the country.

This chapter will be about how decisions are made within that framework. We won't ask how the laws themselves are made—the old saying is that those who like laws or sausages ought not to ask how they are made. And our various levels of government have generated plenty of laws—there is literally no one who comes close to knowing even a tiny fraction of them. There is a joke that God only had ten laws, but even then people couldn't seem to get them straight. There are quite a few more now. The federal Internal Revenue laws comprise some ten thousand pages of dense, inscrutable, and tortured prose, often internally self-contradictory or ambiguous, full of exceptions to exceptions to exceptions, and clearly not written to be understood by even the most literate of the citizenry being taxed. (Occasional newsworthy tests show that the official representatives of the IRS more often than not give wrong answers to real tax questions asked by real citizens.) The Motor Vehicle Code alone of the state of California alone fills fifteen hundred pages of small print with eye-glazing and brain-numbing detail, the California Penal Code fills two thousand pages, and there are lots more where those came from—we are a sorely overgoverned country. And about half of our federal legislators, senators and congressmen, are lawyers, so they and their friends have little incentive to reduce the legal complexity—complexity and ambiguity are money in the bank for lawyers and judges.

The practice of law must once have been different—though George Washington was president of the Constitutional Convention in 1787, more than half the attendees were lawyers. Yet the Constitution is both readable and a marvelous achievement in balancing conflicting interests, while still producing a blueprint for a functioning government. If the government seems dysfunctional now, it is our fault, not theirs.

The growing burden of law is hardly a new problem—there is rarely any strong incentive to repeal a law, and there is a constant itch to proclaim new laws and regulations to meet new or newly perceived problems. It is said that nature abhors a vacuum (a saying that has always struck this author as unusually dumb—since the vast majority of the natural universe is in fact a splendid vacuum, nature must in fact love a vacuum), but any perceived voids in the law books do tend to get filled in due course. The new laws are deemed necessary to resolve the apparent problems of the moment, and are rarely repealed when those problems vanish. There is no constituency for repealing unnecessary laws; laws are repealed only when they cause active grief and generate loud clamor in the vocal population. They are not repealed when they become irrelevant, or apply to so few cases that little would be lost if they were not in the books. (In California, a motor vehicle manufactured before the year 1923 may be licensed as a "Horseless Carriage," but must then be equipped with rear view mirrors, a muffler, and fenders, even if those amenities were not in the original equipment. To how many does that apply?)

Therefore, by a process of accumulation of unchanging law, in a society that is constantly changing, most laws are in fact irrelevant and ignored. Perhaps it is best that way. (There is a saying among corporate managers that any time you reorganize a company you do indeed solve the problem that has been bothering you, at the same time unsolving the problem that was addressed and solved by the previous reorganization. Since it was solved, you've forgotten about it.)

When Byzantine Emperor Justinian I took office in the year 527 A.D., he inherited a thousand years of accretion of Roman law, written over the centuries by generations of energetic jurists, emperors, and assorted other potentates and satraps, and rarely repealed—it was a jungle. It was possible then, just as it is today (and we've only been at it for a couple of hundred years), to find support for defensible legal positions on either side of most questions. Justinian, to his credit, actually decided to do something about it. (Of course, as we mentioned in Chapter 11 about Maria Theresa, if you want to get things done, it helps to be emperor.) Emperor Justinian proclaimed the need for legal reform, summoned his best jurists, set them to work, and the first part of the job was completed in fourteen months. Then another group was appointed to do the rest, and the entire job of overhaul of a thousand years of Roman law was completed by the year 533. It took six years of work by a score of people, and all obsolete laws were then repealed by imperial edict. Compare that with our current situation, where it can take that long to enact a single unimportant law.

The body of law finally promulgated by Justinian has persisted in one form or another in the countries that were once part of the Roman Empire, now known as the civil-law countries. That includes most of Europe—Rome had quite an empire. Such countries are distinguished by a kind of top-down approach to law, in which the actual content of a law is deemed more important than its original rationale. The written law prevails over custom and precedent in such countries.

The contrast is in the common-law countries, where an important ingredient of the law is the body of customs that have grown up with the society, and in which the laws are (at least in part) intended to be a codified expression of accepted common experience. In such countries (Great Britain and the United States are the leading examples) precedent—earlier decisions by other courts, and just plain tradition—are vital to a legal argument, and firm reliance on precedent in interpreting ambiguous laws is important in minimizing the potential for internal contradiction. Thus, the Magna Carta stated that no one can be held responsible for maintaining a bridge *unless* he is legally responsible by ancient custom. The law is not intended to stand by itself; it is intended to reflect community history. Charles Evans Hughes, chief justice of the United States Supreme Court in the 1930s, said that indeed we have a constitution, but "the Constitution is what the judges say it is." The Supreme Court is indeed the court of last resort, and what the Constitution actually says is less important than we were taught in school.

As this is being written a doctor is on trial in Michigan for having done something that violated no written law, but is held by the prosecutors to have violated unwritten common law. That option for prosecutors opens a whole new world.

Obviously the distinction between the two approaches isn't precise. Each of them embodies ingredients of the other, but the underlying philosophies and origins differ. In common-law countries like the United States, law is cumulative for both reasons—judges issue decisions that add to the body of precedent (*case law* is the term used to describe this process), and legislative bodies pass many laws, but repeal few. In addition, in the United States we've had an explosive proliferation of regulatory agencies in the second half of the twentieth century. These agencies issue reams of regulations in their areas of responsibility, regulations that have the force of law. (That's their business—if they didn't issue and enforce regulations, they'd be perceived as failing in their jobs as regulators.) Therefore if, like the Roman

Empire, we persist in this madness for a thousand years—highly unlikely in this author's view—we will have Justinian's problem on an unimaginable scale.

What has this to do with decision making? Everything in the world, because, as we have emphasized throughout the book, you cannot make decisions aimed at achieving an objective without being clear in your mind just what that objective is. Otherwise you fall into the trap so well expressed by the German philosopher who, as quoted by Eugene Wigner, said that philosophy is the misuse of a terminology which was invented for just this purpose. In law, just for one simple example of deliberate fuzziness, we have many references to what a "reasonable person" will do, and we often have the responsibility to behave like one, lest we be punished for breaking the law. That ambiguity (we ourselves are, of course, always reasonable, but our friends are not so consistent, and our enemies never) allows the law to follow the temper of the times without changing the words. Decision making in law has built-in biases that are supposed to reflect societal objectives, and can change without the bother of changing the laws.

Is it more important that an innocent person be set free than that a person truly guilty of a crime be kept from further mischief? Would we rather have a few innocent people suffering in jail, or a few habitual rapists or murderers acquitted and sent back to resume their vocations? In most contested cases there is enough real uncertainty about guilt that either undesirable outcome of a trial is at least conceivable. And each has happened, many times. Our decision rules determine which way we tilt, but we should not comfort ourselves with the fantasy that both unwanted outcomes can be avoided—in the face of genuine uncertainty, that's just not possible. If you want to acquit all the innocent, you will also acquit some of the guilty. If you want to convict all the guilty, you will convict some who are innocent. You can't have it both ways.

Of course, guilt or innocence of a crime is only one type of legal question; we should also talk about other legal decision making, like property rights, so-called civil rights, and a host of other legal decision-making problems. That would be too much law, and would allow this chapter to dominate the book, so we'll pick a couple of illustrative issues and leave the rest to the reader's imagination.

Innocent or Guilty?

In much of ancient history, questions of guilt or innocence were relatively easy to resolve—the gods knew the right answer, so the only problem in finding the real truth was to understand the language of the gods. When God asked Cain, "Where is Abel, thy brother?" it was a rhetorical question, because of course He really knew. (Steven Brams, a student of game theory, has asked why God chose to play that game.) That was, in any event, direct communication. In other societies the gods weren't always so communicative, so it was necessary to either trick them or cajole them, to get them to reveal the facts of the matter. In many ancient societies (and some not so ancient) the priests and other potentates were (and are) supposed to be in direct contact with the gods, so they could serve as intermediaries in these judgments, or could read the signals sent by the gods—there are lots of variations. But there is nowhere in these old arrangements any acknowledgment that there might be genuine uncertainty—that is a relatively new concept for the human race. Since the gods knew, it was only a matter of getting them to tell. A remnant of that view persists in our present practice of requiring witnesses to swear an oath (now secularized into an affirmation), presumably because there is somewhere a higher authority who knows the truth, and who will be offended by lies. Witnesses are presumed to believe that, and therefore to be more motivated to tell the truth when they are under oath. (There are legal penalties for lying under oath, but not for just plain everyday lying—a distinction that has always puzzled this author.)

Procedures such as trial by battle, trial by ordeal, trial by fire, trial by drowning, and even trial by torture, rest on the principle that the gods will make sure that the outcome reflects the truth of the matter in question.

One of the splendid books on this subject is the *Malleus Maleficarum,* written in 1484 to deal with the legal problems associated with the presence of witches in society. The people of that time (despite our egos, they were no less intelligent than we) believed that the Christian world was under attack by Satan, and that his corrupted followers, the witches, were all around us. Given that belief (and our own beliefs will eventually appear similarly misguided) it was clearly a matter of survival to root the witches out—when under attack, one fights back. The stakes were high, the war for our souls was on, and the Inquisition was the result. But it was equally clear, even then, that anyone who was so inclined could settle a private grudge through a false accusation of witchcraft. So it was necessary to be very careful to get at the truth of the matter, to find out whether the accused was really and truly a witch. The two Inquisitors who wrote the book (which was endorsed by the Pope as the authoritative source of wisdom on the subject of witchcraft) went to great lengths to make sure that guilt was firmly established (according to the standards of the time) before the witch was put to death. That there were witches was not in question—the *Malleus* has a long discussion of this point—only whether a particular accused individual was one.

So the purpose of torture was not to wring a confession from an innocent person, it was to test the extent to which she was dominated by Satan. Thus, a person who confesses without torture, or immediately after torture begins, is of course guilty, but prompt confession offers the possibility of redemption. A person who confesses only after severe torture has obviously been helped by the devil, to whom she must therefore be bound. The worst of all are those who never confess, even under severe torture, because that simply cannot be done without complete domination by Satan. Yes, it may seem convoluted reasoning to us, but it was not viewed that way by those who were trying to rid us of witches, and were seeking to identify them by testing the devil's influence. It was all to save Christian civilization. And the *Malleus* says explicitly that "common justice demands that a witch should not be condemned to death unless she is convicted by her own confession." So the confession was important. That's a higher standard for conviction than we now maintain for capital crimes, but of course we're not as good at extracting confessions.

There is a revealing passage in the *Malleus* about trial by red-hot iron. By long tradition, any accused person had the right to demand trial by red-hot iron, in which she (or he) could try to carry a red-hot iron a certain distance. Success meant acquittal. The *Malleus* describes a case in which an accused witch (well known throughout the countryside to be a real witch) demanded the ancient right of trial by red-hot iron. It was, of course, granted—it had to be—and she managed to carry the iron twice as far as was necessary. According to ancient custom she now had to be freed. The writers of the *Malleus* found that outcome a grave miscarriage of justice, since it was inconceivable that the witch could have carried the iron that far without the devil's help, and he, in turn, would not have lent that help unless he greatly prized her allegiance. But she had to be freed, and the right of trial by red-hot iron was no longer recognized for accused witches. That's enough about witches.

Once we break the logical pattern by admitting that the truth about a crime may not be known to any (except perhaps the accused), and that the gods are not going to be of any help, the decision-making problem becomes much harder, and that's where we stand at the end of the twentieth century. In the pure definition of uncertainty we described in Chapter 3, there is uncertainty about whether or not an accused is guilty, and the social problem is how to make the necessary decisions in the face of this uncertainty. Inevitably, as always, that depends on our objectives. One of our methods, in the United States, is to submit the question to a jury.

Juries have an obscure history. They are believed to have first appeared in Charlemagne's time, and to have been brought to England by the Normans. Their use in the English-speaking countries is often traced to the Magna Carta (1215 A.D.), but in fact there is nothing in the Magna Carta about juries. It does declare that some punishments may not be imposed, except "by the oath of honest men of the neighborhood," but that is a judicial role. The same document states that misbehavior by earls and barons may only be punished through their peers, but that is peer review, and again not a jury trial.

Whatever its origin, the idea took hold about five hundred years ago, and grew slowly in Western Europe, then crossed the Channel to England, from which it spread to the United States (then colonies of England). Then it declined in popularity in the rest of the world, but kept growing here. Jury trials have been either abandoned or are on the way out in most civilized countries, with the single unfortunate exception of the United States. Lawyers love them, and the trial lawyers' associations are heavy contributors to legislators who block improvement. The right to trial by an impartial jury is explicit in our constitution, and 90 percent of all jury trials held in the entire world are held in the United States. Despite popular belief, fostered in the schools, the Constitution *does not* say anything about any right to a jury of our peers; it requires only that the jury be impartial. Subsequent requirements that a jury be representative of the community, and that defendants have a role in selecting the jury that tries them, are also not in the Constitution. (They would probably have been laughed out of the Constitutional Convention). More than a hundred thousand jury trials are held each year in the United States—no other country comes close. And there is no other country known to this author in which a defendant has the right to help pick the jury that will try him. Shopping for the right jury is a major component of preparation for trial in the United States. If pursuit of the truth and determination of the facts are the real objectives of a jury trial, that sounds nutty to the author, but it must already be clear that he is not a lawyer.

There has been a major and fundamental change in the character of juries in the United States in the past few decades. Up to quite recently, the criteria for jury selection were largely the constitutional ones, above all the requirement for impartiality, and there were no constraints against seeking competent jurors, even jurors who might know something about the subject in dispute. As a matter of practice federal judicial districts (there are ninety-four in the country) followed the practices of the states in which they were located, and standards varied widely among the states. But in 1968 the Congress passed a law requiring that federal juries be "selected at random from a fair cross section of the community." That was a law, and is not in the Constitution. Therefore, starting in 1969 in the federal courts, and spreading rapidly to the rest of the system, we have had far greater emphasis on proportional representation on juries, to the point at which competence and knowledge are in practice considered disqualifying handicaps. It is the perceived job of the lawyers for each side to convince the jury that their view of the facts is correct, so it is clearly in the best interests of the lawyers to have a jury that can be persuaded, which is to say hoodwinked. That is best done with jurors whose minds are uncluttered by knowledge or understanding of the subject in dispute. Or indeed, if truth be told, of more than a working minimum of intelligence or education. (This author freely admits to the shame of being a professor, and even to the worse shame of having a Ph.D.—the price of youthful indiscretion—so he is instantly rejected for jury service when the facts are made known to the lawyers in the case. If not by one side, then surely by the other—it depends on which one has the weaker case, and therefore places more value on confusing the jury. Of course, the lawyers overrate the title and the degree, but what do they know?) The Supreme Court has ruled (again, it is not in the Constitution) that the lawyers may not dismiss a juror for reasons of race, gender, or religious affiliation, but education doesn't rate this same protection. The result of this fundamental change, and fundamental it is, has been a dramatic decline in confidence in the system by a large fraction of the population, fueled in part by some notoriously indefensible jury decisions in both criminal and civil cases. Jury decisions, ostensibly resolving disputes about fact, may not be reviewed by any court in the nation, according to the Constitution. They are final.

During this transition from impartiality and fact-finding to equal representation and indifference as objectives for a jury, there have been notable milestones, but one that will always stay fixed in this author's memory is the spectacle of a United States senator speaking in support of a nominee for appointment to the United States Supreme Court, the highest court in the land. This nominee had been widely criticized for being what we would now call intellectually challenged. He just didn't appear to be very smart (in fairness, appearances can be deceiving), yet the senator defended the president's choice by acknowledging that the candidate might be mediocre, but then declaring that even mediocre people deserve representation on the Supreme Court. It seems silly (downright hilarious), but once you start down the road of requiring that a jury be a cross section of the community, why not extend the idea to judges? This is an important change in criteria, and that argument now extends to many job qualification lists—the right of everyone to a job takes precedence over the employer's former right to seek the best-qualified person for a job. The price we will pay for this is not yet known, but there will be one.

A jury is used only to decide facts in dispute, not to interpret law, though the roles are inevitably intertwined. One might naively think that the question of objectives, of which we have made so much in this book, would not be relevant to the determination of facts, but to think that would be wrong. When there is uncertainty about facts, different outcomes are possible, and the decision can be pushed in any direction by an inherent bias. The word *bias* has gotten a bad name, but all it means is a leaning in one direction. The leaning may or may not be justified by other considerations.

For example, in the question of innocence or guilt we have made a societal decision to favor the verdict of not guilty in a criminal case, and have done so by placing the burden of proof on the prosecution—you are presumed innocent until actually proven guilty. By contrast, in your dealings with the Internal Revenue Service, you are guilty unless you can prove yourself innocent—if you claim a deduction, you had better be prepared to prove it, since your solemn oath is not enough. If a traffic policeman charges you with exceeding the speed limit or rolling through a stop sign, and you swear you didn't do anything of the kind, it is a polite fiction that the burden of proof is on him. It is on you.

So we instruct juries in criminal cases that they should return a verdict of not guilty (which is not the same as innocent), unless the prosecution has satisfied them, beyond a reasonable doubt, that the defendant is indeed guilty. Those words are a deliberate attempt to tilt the playing field, and reflect a judgment (often not shared by the victims of violent crime) that it is better to turn a guilty person loose to sin again, than to imprison an innocent one. If that principle is applied to habitual perpetrators of the more heinous crimes against individuals, few people on the street will actually agree. But those are our laws. This author has tried asking friends if they think that a person who has been accused of rape, with an even-money chance that he is guilty, should be turned loose. (Most rapists have done it before—it is not a once-in-a-lifetime crime.) According to our customs he should be turned loose, since 50-50 certainly implies reasonable doubt. Most people are nervous about the question, and would rather not face it, but when pressed would like to apply different standards of proof for different crimes. For crimes like rape or mugging, where a person who has done it once is very likely to do it again, most people would like to err on the safe side, conviction, whereas lesser crimes, not against people, bring out the merciful in us. Our laws make no such distinction.

Our present system requires us to define reasonable doubt in simple terms, because it is unthinkable to have such an unfamiliar concept as probability in a courtroom. And truly, in the hands of judges and lawyers, it could be a disaster. (In a federal case in which the author once testified on behalf of the government, the judge said in open court that he wasn't interested in probability, because if he were he would be acting as a bookie, and "this Court is not a bookie." In the great book of silly comments, that's a winner, and he was soon overturned by the Supreme Court.) But since we can't talk about probability, the proper language for dealing with decision making under uncertainty, what do we do about reasonable doubt? We handle the subject through circumlocutions and portentous and polysyllabic but meaningless words. Remember the German philosopher mentioned above.

In most courts the choice of the proper words to define reasonable doubt is deemed too important to be left to the judge, and is prescribed by higher authority, presumably after long deliberation by legal savants. Here is the exact prescribed definition in California—it's similar in other states:

> Reasonable doubt is defined as follows: It is not a mere possible doubt; because everything relating to human affairs, and depending on moral evidence, is open to some possible or imaginary doubt. It is that state of the case which, after the entire comparison and consideration of all the evidence, leaves the minds of the jurors in that condition that they cannot say they feel an abiding conviction, to a moral certainty, of the truth of the charge.

That sure does help, doesn't it? You don't have to be certain, just morally certain. This drivel has to be read, verbatim, to the jury in a criminal trial in California. It is the price we pay for not allowing odds to be mentioned in court, and is one reason for the well-known unpredictability of trial juries.

So if we want to sometimes convict the innocent, torture is one way to go, and is still widely practiced in the ostensibly civilized world. If we prefer to turn the guilty loose, our present system is pretty good at that. But we can't have it both ways.

Precision

All of decision making centers on the problem of making specific decisions in the face of uncertainties—whether about facts, or probabilities, or utilities, or whatever. The uncertainties are part of the package that goes into the decision. That is also true of the problem of guilt discussed in the last section—the laws are sufficiently broad, and the facts sufficiently unclear, to make the question of guilt or innocence difficult—uncertainty abounds.

There is another way to resolve many of the uncertainties, by writing the law itself with enforcement in mind. You can build guilt into the law by writing it so simply that proof of guilt is as easy as possible, and can do that by, in effect, sacrificing the law's social purpose to its enforceability.

For example, most speed limits on highways are supposed to be surrogates for safety. Obviously there is no magically safe speed on any highway for all drivers, for all vehicles, and for all traffic and road conditions. Nor is there any agreed standard for how safe the highways ought to be—one of our many silly fantasies is that if we only tried harder we could eliminate highway accidents. The main purpose of that fantasy is to relieve us of the agony of deciding how much safety we do want—and what we are willing to give up to achieve it. And there is no exact speed that always and precisely divides the safe from the dangerous. As all drivers know, there are many other variables—some drivers can't handle forty miles per hour while others do well at much higher speeds. Many speed laws (but not all) recognize this by permitting a speeding driver to claim (and try to prove) that he was in fact driving both fast and safely. (Don't try it—you have a negligible chance of winning in court, despite the law.) There are some absolute speed limits for which no exceptions apply, the basic speed laws. The entire United States had such a no-holds-barred speed limit of fifty-five miles per hour for twenty years. True, it began as a means of conserving gasoline after the first Arab oil embargo of 1974–75 (there will be others), but was retained for ostensible safety reasons for twenty years after that. (Before the nationwide limit was imposed there were some states that had no speed limits at all—the law only required prudence. It is much harder to prove that a driver is driving imprudently than to measure his speed, so law enforcement officials much prefer absolute speed limits. It is decision avoidance, not collision avoidance, that drives speed limits.)

We mentioned that horseless carriages in California must have fenders, rearview mirrors, and mufflers. Why not the full suite of safety equipment? Why not a limit on their noisiness, instead of a requirement for a muffler of unspecified effectiveness? Well, you can see mirrors, fenders, and mufflers, but you can't see noise. As another example, it is clearly unsafe to drive with an obstructed windshield, but how much obstruction does it take to make trouble? In California (forgive the author for harping on his state—the California code is handy, and other states have similar rules) it is legal to obstruct a square five inches on a side on the lower corner of the windshield nearest the driver, but the obstructed square can be seven inches across on the other side. We all know that for some windshields and for some drivers (especially very short ones) a five-inch square is too much obstruction, while a very tall driver never even notices that part of the windshield. But the rule as written is easy to enforce. It avoids decision making in court, though it bears little connection to its purported purpose.

All through the law books one will find laws and rules written to facilitate enforcement, providing sharp boundaries for what is in fact the very fuzzy line that divides right from wrong. This is fundamentally bad for a democracy, because in fact it hands to the law enforcement agencies the decision-making process that ought to belong to the judicial system—it promotes discrimination. During the last months of the fifty-five-mile-per-hour speed limit hardly any drivers were in fact obeying the law, and that meant that the police could select any car or driver for enforcement, according to their own private preferences. It is well known among drivers of small sports cars that they are subject to discriminatory enforcement, as are young drivers and drivers of brightly colored cars.

But precise laws, however ill-considered, do relieve the need for decision making in law. It's one way out.

Complex Matters

Matters like guilt or innocence are important but simple in form—like a true-false test. But some legal questions are not—was there a valid contract? are pesticides dangerous? was that particular lung cancer caused by cigarette smoking? was the bridge badly designed or was its collapse caused by the flood? were those warts caused by eating too much chocolate on Valentine's Day? and so forth. Juries make important decisions in those matters too, and the lawyers have their fun every time it happens. Honorable lawyers will tell you that it is the function of a lawyer to help the jury or the court to follow the truth, wherever it may lead, but lawyers with that as their prime objective will soon have few clients. Most lawyers will tell you that their real obligation is to present the best possible case for the clients who are paying them—quite a different goal. And some disputes decided by jurors involve matters so complex that no one in the courtroom—judge, lawyers, or jury—comes into the matter with any knowledge of the subject. (Any potential juror with such skills will soon be dismissed.) It is a kind of vanity that leads to the belief (sanctified in 1993 in a memorable Supreme Court decision on the effects of a drug) that a judge has the capacity to deal responsibly with any subject that comes up before him. The Supreme Court said nothing about lawyers and jurors. Besides, the Court that wrote that decision is made up of judges, who are in real life lawyers.

This is such a long subject that we can't possibly do it justice here (see the marvelous book *Galileo's Revenge,* by Peter Huber, for the flavor). The temptation to write too much is enormous: the 1925 Scopes trial in Tennessee, many trials on the validity of scientific evidence, fluoridation, cancer remedies, airplane accidents, DNA evidence, asbestos, and so forth. Decision making on complex issues involving law and government is a mess. Read Huber, then go forth and multiply.

The problem is that if a subject is complex, it is complex. What the word means is that it isn't simple, which means that it can't be explained in words of one syllable, even to a willing and eager listener. This author has been a physics professor for most of his life, and knows from first-hand experience that physics is not an easy subject to teach, even under the best circumstances. But imagine trying to do it in a classroom in which there is a person whose job it is to debunk everything you say, to distort the things he doesn't debunk, to lie with impunity, to make no secret of his loathing for you, and to urge the students that, say, tea leaves are a better way to predict eclipses. All this to a class of students specifically chosen to have no prior background, and instructed to give the opposing views equal weight. (We sometimes call such an event a balanced debate, in the same sense that horse-and-rabbit stew is made with one horse and one rabbit.) In our legislatures we have a sufficiently cumbersome system of checks and balances to keep things under some minimal control, but not in the courts. (Even in legislatures, we have the spectacles of the Indiana Legislature almost passing the 1897 law we mentioned in Chapter 14, the Tennessee law that led to the Scopes trial, and the decisions by the governing bodies of any number of states and localities—including Los Angeles—to deny the benefits of fluoridation to their hapless children. In some of these cases it is because of active efforts by uneducated zealots, in others even that isn't necessary—the legislators are up to the job without help.)

There is still a Flat Earth Society, so imagine the existence of a Bibipent Society, devoted to the notion that $2 + 2 = 5$. Such a society might well have filed suit to stop the schools from teaching $2 + 2 = 4$ as if it were a fact, and require them to present it as "only theory," with $2 + 2 = 5$ as an alternative possibility, deserving equal time. They would doubtless say that the purpose of a school is to educate, not to indoctrinate. (Does all this sound familiar? That's the way it is with creationism and evolution.) It wouldn't be hard to find a reference somewhere, or even a hired gun, willing to take the position that that $2 + 2$ really equals 5. (Experts come with different levels of expertise, and different fees. And the 1993 Supreme Court decision we mentioned above gave wide latitude to the judge in selecting what expert testimony to allow in court. In the case of the circumference of a circle there is even a biblical reference that sets it equal to three times the diameter—not as wrong as the proposed Indiana value of pi, but still very wrong.) So, in this imaginary scenario about 2 plus 2, the defense calls a renowned Princeton physicist/mathematician to the stand (call him Dr. E.), and the following exchange takes place:

—Doctor, when did you first come to believe that two plus two make four?

—Oh, I've known that since I was a child.

—Did your teachers prove it to you, or did they just tell you to believe them, to take it on faith?

—Well, it's not easy to prove such things in elementary school. When you start learning mathematics, some things need to be memorized.

—So they just made you swallow it. And did they learn it from their teachers?

  —Objection, hearsay.

  —Sustained. Confine yourself to what he knows as an expert.

—Well then, Doctor, did your teachers tell you about the alternative theories?

—No (getting angry) there are no alternative theories worthy of the name.

—Come now, Doctor, we are here today because there are good people who believe otherwise, and they have rights, too.

—I'm sorry for them, because they are being misled.

—Well then, Doctor, if you're so sure of yourself, could you prove to this good jury that two plus two make four? We'd all like to hear you try.

—We don't use the word *prove* in mathematics the way you do in court.

—So you can't do it. Well, Doctor, have you ever heard of Peano's postulates?

—Of course. They are a set of postulates that underly the mathematical system of natural integers.

—Very good, Doctor. So in a manner of speaking the quaint notion that two plus two make four depends on them?

—Well, it can be developed from them, yes.

—And can you prove those postulates for the jury?
They're listening.
—I've already told you that prove means . . .
—Yes, yes, Doctor. Did Peano prove these so-called pos-
tulates, whoever he was?
—Of course not. They are postulates, and you don't
prove postulates. Postulates are what you assume in or-
der to prove theorems.
—I see. You teach all this to innocent children, but it's
all assumptions, and you can't prove it?
—[Judge] Doctor, Doctor, put down that gavel. Restrain
yourself.

It's not as far-fetched as you might think. Questions about
whether certain chemicals "cause" cancer, or how DNA evidence
should be interpreted, or whether a structural failure was due to
materials or design, are all decided by juries under similar conditions. Where it really matters to us, as in choosing a surgeon to
remove an inflamed appendix, we tend to forsake democracy for
expertise. But not in jury trials.

23

Intro Redux

So where are we? We said at the beginning that the book would proceed from simple decisions by an individual who knew all the facts, through group problems, and on into areas in which we simply don't know consistent ways to make optimal decisions for either the whole society, or for those individuals involved. The dating game we started with is in the first category, and all the issues of government are in the last. But we've tried to emphasize some features that are common to all these problems, and it might be useful to restate them. (It's a little chancy to do this, since we are all tempted to oversimplify life, especially in this era in which sound bites substitute for news, docudramas for history, and book reviews for books.) So you shouldn't believe that what follows is a summary of the book.

Rational decisions are impossible unless you make clear at the outset just what it is that you want to accomplish, and what you want to avoid. This applies to both individual and group decisions, though it's obviously harder for the latter.

If you can also set a value on the possible consequences, plus or minus, and couple that value with the odds on a particular outcome, that combination gives you all you need to make a rational decision.

Even a solidly rational decision can turn out wrong (and vice versa), so there is no reason for wallowing in guilt or self-loathing if things go unexpectedly wrong, or for preening if you luck out. If an outcome is uncertain, it is uncertain, and all you can ever do is play the odds. You'll win more often than you lose if you play the odds with intelligence.

A sure road to bad decisions is to separate the decision makers from the beneficiaries, the deciders from the decidees, so to speak, as in representation without taxation, and juries. Though people pontificate about their concern for the welfare of society, that concern is most visible when it can be displayed at no cost to them personally. Altruism runs for shelter when it imposes unpleasant costs.

Some kind of understanding of probability, at some level, is essential for rational decision making. The more the better. And it's not that hard to get used to it.

Group decisions are fundamentally harder to keep rational than are individual decisions, and there is plenty of room in the machinery of group decision making for manipulation and chicanery. No known electoral method is immune to this, but some have more resistance to the disease than others.

There is no satisfactory way to translate individual preferences into a group preference, free of unwanted consequences—that is Arrow's theorem, and is incontrovertibly true. Therefore every voting method has flaws, and the most desirable in any situation is the one with the flaws that will do the least damage.

It is not necessarily true that group decisions aimed at majority approval are beneficial for the majority, or for the society as a whole. Nor is it true that anyone knows a satisfactory solution to that basic problem. The schools teach otherwise, and it is ultimately counterproductive to do so. Better to know your problems than to pretend that they don't exist. Any psychiatrist can tell you that.

As a corollary, the myth that if everyone's behavior is governed by enlightened self-interest, the outcome will be favorable for the society, is just that, a myth. It is also unfortunately a myth that serves as camouflage for the efffects of unenlightened self-interest.

Though some of these ideas find their way into our private decision making, at some visceral level, many of our public policies seem to be organized around the mistaken assumption that none of the above is true.

And as a corollary of that, no entirely satisfactory form of government, in the form of group decision making for the benefit of society, has yet been invented by the human race. The fable that proclaims ours as representing that ultimate invention is another myth. The fact that we don't know anything closer is irrelevant to the first point.

If you want to gamble, play at sports, invest in the stock market, select a spouse, or make war, it is a good idea to know what you are doing.

Decision making at all levels, and in all areas, can be improved by knowledge. We hope this book has contributed just a bit to that knowledge. We also hope you enjoyed reading it.

Index